OFFICIAL BASEBALL RULES

2024 Edition

Official Baseball Rules
2024 Edition

JOINT COMPETITION COMMITTEE

Corbin Burnes
Bill DeWitt
Zac Gallen
Greg Johnson

Whit Merrifield
Bill Miller
Dick Monfort
Mark Shapiro

Austin Slater
John Stanton, Chair
Tom Werner

———————•———————

Committee Secretary
Paul V. Mifsud, Jr.

Editors
Vanish Grover
Raquel Wagner

———————•———————

Cover photo by Daniel Shirley/MLB Photos.

ISBN 978-1-63727-386-9

Printed in the United States of America

FOREWORD

This code of rules governs the playing of baseball games by professional teams of Major League Baseball and any league within the professional development league system operated by Major League Baseball in which Minor League Clubs are assigned to compete.

We recognize that many amateur and non-professional organizations play their games under professional rules and we are happy to make our rules available as widely as possible. It is well to remember that specifications as to fields, equipment, etc., may be modified to meet the needs of each group.

Money fines, long-term suspensions and similar penalties imposed by this code are not practicable for amateur groups, but officers and umpires of such organizations should insist on strict observance of all the rules governing the playing of the game.

IMPORTANT NOTES

(1) The Playing Rules Committee, at its December 2014 meeting, voted to reorganize and recodify the Official Baseball Rules into a more logical and organized manner. No wording or language was changed (other than the amendments made for that year); only the order and placement of the rules were modified. In this edition Comments to the Official Rules are highlighted in a shaded box rather than being printed in smaller typeface as had been the case prior to 2015.

(2) The Playing Rules Committee, at its December 1977 meeting, voted to incorporate the Notes/Case Book/Comments section directly into the Official Baseball Rules at the appropriate places. Basically, the Case Book interprets or elaborates on the basic rules and in essence have the same effect as rules when applied to particular sections for which they are intended.

This arrangement is designed to give quicker access to any written language pertaining to an Official Rule and does not require a reader to refer to different sections of the Official Baseball Rules book in considering the application of a particular rule.

Case Book material in this edition are in shaded boxes and are labeled as "Comment."

Summary of Rule Changes for 2024

- Amended Rule 2.01 to reflect the updated dimensions of the grass line of the infield dirt in fair territory along the first base line.

- Amended Rule 5.09(a)(11) to reflect the updated dimensions governing certain interference calls for throw at first base.

- Amended Rule 5.10(g) to reflect that a pitcher who warms up on the field at the start of the inning is required to pitch to at least the first batter of the inning until such batter is put out or reaches first base.

- Amended Rule 5.10(m) to update the number of mound visits each team is allowed through nine innings.

- Amended the *Penalty for Interference* in Rule 6.01(a) to reflect the updated dimensions governing certain interference calls for throws at first base.

- Amended Rule 7.01 to clarify the policies surrounding regulation games.

- Amended Rule 7.02 to clarify the policies surrounding suspended games.

- Amended "A Called Game" in the Definition of Terms to clarify the Office of the Commissioner's role in terminating play.

- Added "A Postponed Game" to the Definition of Terms.

Table of Contents
2024 Official Baseball Rules

5.00—PLAYING THE GAME

1.00–OBJECTIVES OF THE GAME

1.01 Baseball is a game between two teams of nine players each, under direction of a manager, played on an enclosed field in accordance with these rules, under jurisdiction of one or more umpires.

1.02 The offensive team's objective is to have its batter become a runner, and its runners advance.

1.03 The defensive team's objective is to prevent offensive players from becoming runners, and to prevent their advance around the bases.

1.04 When a batter becomes a runner and touches all bases legally he shall score one run for his team.

1.05 The objective of each team is to win by scoring more runs than the opponent.

1.06 The winner of the game shall be that team which shall have scored, in accordance with these rules, the greater number of runs at the conclusion of a regulation game.

2.00–THE PLAYING FIELD

2.01 Layout of the Field

The field shall be laid out according to the instructions below, supplemented by the diagrams in Appendices 1, 2, and 3.

The infield shall be a 90-foot square. The outfield shall be the area between two foul lines formed by extending two sides of the square, as in diagram in Appendix 1 (page 156). The distance from home base to the nearest fence, stand or other obstruction on fair territory shall be 250 feet or more. A distance of 320 feet or more along the foul lines, and 400 feet or more to center field is preferable. The infield shall be graded so that the base lines and home plate are level. The pitcher's plate shall be 10 inches above the level of home plate. The degree of slope from a point 6 inches in front of the pitcher's plate to a point 6 feet toward home plate shall be 1 inch to 1 foot, and such degree of slope shall be uniform. The infield and outfield, including the boundary lines, are fair territory and all other area is foul territory.

It is desirable that the line from home base through the pitcher's plate to second base shall run East-Northeast.

It is recommended that the distance from home base to the backstop, and from the base lines to the nearest fence, stand or other obstruction on foul territory shall be 60 feet or more. *See* Appendix 1.

When location of home base is determined, with a steel tape measure 127 feet, 3⅜ inches in desired direction to establish second base. From home base, measure 90 feet toward first base; from second base, measure 90 feet toward first base; the intersection of these lines establishes first base. From home base, measure 90 feet toward third base; from second base, measure 90 feet toward third base; the intersection of these lines establishes third base. The distance between first base and third base is 127 feet, 3⅜ inches. All measurements from home base shall be taken from the point where the first and third base lines intersect.

The catcher's box, the batters' boxes, the coaches' boxes, the three-foot first base lines and the next batter's boxes shall be laid out as shown in the diagrams in Appendices 1 and 2.

The foul lines and all other playing lines indicated in the diagrams by solid black lines shall be marked with paint or non-toxic and non-burning chalk or other white material.

The grass lines and dimensions shown on the diagrams are those used in many fields, but they are not mandatory and each Club shall determine the size and shape of the grassed and bare areas of its playing field, except as follows:

(a) The grass line of the outer boundary of the infield dirt shall be a 95-foot radius from the center of the pitcher's plate. A Club will be considered to be in compliance with this provision if the average distance of the grass line of the outer boundary of the infield dirt is less than 96 feet but more than 94 feet, and no individual measurement is more than 96 feet or less than 94 feet.

(b) The grass line of the infield dirt in fair territory along the first base line between home and first base shall be no less than 18 inches and no more than 24 inches from the first base line.

NOTE: (a) Any Playing Field constructed by a professional Club after June 1, 1958, shall provide a minimum distance of 325 feet from home base to the nearest fence, stand or other obstruction on the right and left field foul lines, and a minimum distance of 400 feet to the center field fence.

(b) No existing playing field shall be remodeled after June 1, 1958, in such manner as to reduce the distance from home base to the foul poles and to the center field fence below the minimum specified in paragraph (a) above.

2.02 Home Base

Home base shall be marked by a five-sided slab of whitened rubber. It shall be a 17-inch square with two of the corners removed so that one edge is 17 inches long, two adjacent sides are 8½ inches and the remaining two sides are 12 inches and set at an angle to make a point. It shall be set in the ground with the point at the intersection of the lines extending from home base to first base and to third base; with the 17-inch edge facing the pitcher's plate, and the two 12-inch edges coinciding with the first and third base lines. The top edges of home base shall be beveled and the base shall be fixed in the ground level with the ground surface. (*See* drawing D in Appendix 2.)

2.03 The Bases

First, second and third bases shall be marked by white canvas or rubber-covered bags, securely attached to the ground as indicated in Diagram 2. The first and third base bags shall be entirely within the infield. The second base bag shall be centered on second base. The bags shall be 18 inches square, not less than three nor more than five inches thick, and filled with soft material.

2.04 The Pitcher's Plate

The pitcher's plate shall be a rectangular slab of whitened rubber, 24 inches by 6 inches. It shall be set in the ground as shown in Diagrams 1 and 2, so that the distance between the pitcher's plate and home base (the rear point of home plate) shall be 60 feet, 6 inches.

2.05 Benches

The home Club shall furnish players' benches, one each for the home and visiting teams. Such benches shall not be less than twenty-five feet from the base lines. They shall be roofed and shall be enclosed at the back and ends.

3.00–EQUIPMENT AND UNIFORMS

3.01 The Ball

The ball shall be a sphere formed by yarn wound around a small core of cork, rubber or similar material, covered with two strips of white horsehide or cowhide, tightly stitched together. It shall weigh not less than five nor more than 5¼ ounces avoirdupois and measure not less than nine nor more than 9¼ inches in circumference.

No player shall intentionally discolor or damage the ball by rubbing it with soil, rosin, paraffin, licorice, sand-paper, emery- paper or other foreign substance.

PENALTY: The umpire shall demand the ball and remove the offender from the game. In addition, the offender shall be suspended automatically for 10 games. For rules in regard to a pitcher defacing the ball, *see* Rules 6.02(c)(2) through (6).

Rule 3.01 Comment: Should a ball come partially apart in a game, it is in play until the play is completed.

3.02 The Bat

(a) The bat shall be a smooth, round stick not more than 2.61 inches in diameter at the thickest part and not more than 42 inches in length. The bat shall be one piece of solid wood.

NOTE: No laminated or experimental bats shall be used in a professional game (either championship season or exhibition games) until the manufacturer has secured approval from Major League Baseball of his design and methods of manufacture.

(b) Cupped Bats. An indentation in the end of the bat up to 1¼ inches in depth is permitted and may be no wider than two inches and no less than one inch in diameter. The indentation must be curved with no foreign substance added.

(c) The bat handle, for not more than 18 inches from its end, may be covered or treated with any material or substance to improve the grip. Any such material or substance that extends past the 18-inch limitation shall cause the bat to be removed from the game.

NOTE: If the umpire discovers that the bat does not conform to (c) above until a time during or after which the bat has been used in play, it shall not be grounds for declaring the batter out, or ejected from the game.

Rule 3.02(c) Comment: If pine tar extends past the 18-inch limitation, then the umpire, on his own initiative or if alerted by the opposing team, shall order the batter to use a different bat. The batter may use the bat later in the game only if the excess substance is removed. If no objections are raised prior to a bat's use, then a violation of Rule 3.02(c) on that play does not nullify any action or play on the field.

(d) No colored bat may be used in a professional game unless approved by Major League Baseball.

3.03 Player Uniforms

(a) All players on a team shall wear uniforms identical in color, trim and style, and all players' uniforms shall include minimal six-inch numbers on their backs.

(b) Any part of an undershirt exposed to view shall be of a uniform solid color for all players on a team. Any player other than the pitcher may have numbers, and/or letters, insignia attached to the sleeve of the undershirt.

(c) No player whose uniform does not conform to that of his teammates shall be permitted to participate in a game.

(d) A league may provide that each team shall wear a distinctive uniform at all times, or that each team shall have two sets of uniforms, white for home games and a different color for road games.

(e) Sleeve lengths may vary for individual players, but the sleeves of each individual player shall be approximately the same length; no player shall wear ragged, frayed or slit sleeves; and no pitcher shall wear sleeves that are white, gray, nor, in the judgment of an umpire, distracting in any manner.

(f) No player shall attach to his uniform tape or other material of different color from his uniform.

(g) No part of the uniform shall include a pattern that imitates or suggests the shape of a baseball.

(h) Glass buttons and polished metal shall not be used on a uniform.

(i) No player shall attach anything to the heel or toe of his shoe other than the ordinary shoe plate or toe plate. Shoes with pointed spikes similar to golf or track shoes shall not be worn.

(j) No part of the uniform shall include patches or designs relating to commercial advertisements. Notwithstanding the foregoing or anything else in these Rules, a Club may license to third-party commercial sponsors the right to place their name, logos and/or marks on the uniform, provided that the patch or design is approved in advance by the Office of the Commissioner after consultation with the Players Association.

(k) A league may provide that the uniforms of its member teams include the names of its players on their backs. Any name other than the last name of the player must be approved by the Office of the Commissioner. If adopted, all uniforms for a team must have the names of its players.

3.04 Catcher's Mitt

The catcher may wear a leather mitt not more than thirty-eight inches in circumference, nor more than fifteen and one-half inches from top to bottom. Such limits shall include all lacing and any leather band or facing attached to the outer edge of the mitt. The space between the thumb section and the finger section of the mitt shall not exceed six inches at the top of the mitt and four inches at the base of the thumb crotch. The web shall measure not more than seven inches across the top or more than six inches from its top to the base of the thumb crotch. The web may be either a lacing, lacing through leather tunnels, or a center piece of leather which may be an extension of the palm, connected to the mitt with lacing and constructed so that it will not exceed any of the above mentioned measurements.

3.05 First Baseman's Glove

The first baseman may wear a leather glove or mitt not more than thirteen inches long from top to bottom and not more than eight inches wide across the palm, measured from the base of the thumb crotch to the outer edge of the mitt. The space between the thumb section and the finger section of the mitt shall not exceed four inches at the top of the mitt and three and one-half inches at the base of the thumb crotch. The mitt shall be constructed so that this space is permanently fixed and cannot be enlarged, extended, widened, or deepened by the use of any materials or process whatsoever. The web of the mitt shall measure not more than five inches from its top to the base of the thumb crotch. The web may be either a lacing, lacing through leather tunnels, or a center piece of leather which may be an extension of the palm connected to the mitt with lacing and constructed so that it will not exceed the above mentioned measurements. The webbing shall not be constructed of wound or wrapped lacing or deepened to make a net type of trap. The glove may be of any weight.

3.06 Fielding Gloves

Each fielder, other than the catcher, may use or wear a leather glove. The measurements covering size of glove shall be made by measuring front side or ball receiving side of glove. The tool or measuring tape shall be placed to contact the surface or feature of item being measured and follow all contours in the process. The glove shall not measure more than 13 inches from the tip of any one of the 4 fingers, through the ball pocket to the bottom edge or heel of glove. The glove shall not measure more than 7¾ inches wide, measured from the inside seam at base of first finger, along base of other fingers, to the outside edge of little finger edge of glove. The space or area between the thumb and first finger, called crotch, may be filled with leather webbing or back stop. The webbing may be constructed of two plies of standard leather to close the crotch area entirely, or it may be constructed of a series of tunnels made of leather, or a series of panels of leather, or of lacing leather thongs. The webbing may not be constructed of wound or wrapped lacing to make a net type of trap. When webbing is made to cover entire crotch area, the webbing can be constructed so as to be flexible. When constructed of a series of sections, they must be joined together. These sections may not be so constructed to allow depression to be developed by curvatures in the section sides. The webbing shall be made to control the size of the crotch opening. The crotch opening shall measure not more than 4½ inches at the top, not more than 5¾ inches deep, and shall be 3½ inches wide at its bottom. The opening of the crotch shall not be more than 4½ inches at any point below its top. The webbing shall be secured at each side, and at top and bottom of crotch. The attachment is to be made with leather lacing, these connections to be secured. If they stretch or become loose, they shall be adjusted to their proper condition. The glove can be of any weight. *See* Appendix 4 for diagram of glove dimensions.

3.07 Pitcher's Glove

(a) The pitcher's glove may not, exclusive of piping, be white, gray, nor, in the judgment of an umpire, distracting in any manner. No fielder, regardless of position, may use a fielding glove that falls within a PANTONE® color set lighter than the current 14-series.

(b) No pitcher shall attach to his glove any foreign material of a color different from the glove.

(c) The umpire-in-chief shall cause a glove that violates Rules 3.07(a) or (b) to be removed from the game, either on his own initiative, at the recommendation of another umpire or upon complaint of the opposing manager that the umpire-in-chief agrees has merit.

3.08 Helmets

A Professional League shall adopt the following rule pertaining to the use of helmets:

(a) All players shall use some type of protective helmet while at bat and while running the bases.

(b) All players in the Minor Leagues shall wear a double ear-flap helmet while at bat.

(c) All Major League players must wear a single ear-flap helmet (or at the player's option, a double ear-flap helmet).

(d) All catchers shall wear a catcher's protective helmet and face mask while receiving a pitch.

(e) All base coaches shall wear a protective helmet while performing their duties.

(f) All bat/ball boys or girls shall wear a double ear-flap protective helmet while performing their duties.

Rule 3.08 Comment: If the umpire observes any violation of these rules, he shall direct the violation to be corrected. If the violation is not corrected within a reasonable time, in the umpire's judgment, the umpire shall eject the offender from the game, and disciplinary action, as appropriate, will be recommended.

3.09 Undue Commercialization

Playing equipment including but not limited to the bases, pitcher's plate, baseball, bats, uniforms, catcher's mitts, first baseman's gloves, infielders' and outfielders' gloves and protective helmets, as detailed in the provisions of this rule, shall not contain any undue commercialization of the product. Designations by the manufacturer on any such equipment must be in good taste as to the size and content of the manufacturer's logo or the brand name of the item. The provisions of this Rule 3.09 shall apply to professional leagues only.

NOTE: Manufacturers who plan innovative changes in baseball equipment for professional baseball leagues should submit same to Major League Baseball prior to production.

3.10 Equipment on the Field

(a) Members of the offensive team shall carry all gloves and other equipment off the field and to the dugout while their team is at bat. No equipment shall be left lying on the field, either in fair or foul territory.

(b) The use of any markers on the field that create a tangible reference system on the field is prohibited.

4.00–GAME PRELIMINARIES

4.01 Umpire Duties

Before the game begins the umpire shall:

(a) Require strict observance of all rules governing implements of play and equipment of players;

(b) Be sure that all playing lines (heavy lines on Appendices No. 1 and No.2) are marked with lime, chalk or other white material easily distinguishable from the ground or grass;

(c) Receive from the home Club a supply of regulation baseballs, the number and make to be certified to the home Club by the Office of the Commissioner. The umpire shall inspect the baseballs and ensure they are regulation baseballs and that they are properly rubbed so that the gloss is removed. The umpire shall be the sole judge of the fitness of the balls to be used in the game;

(d) Be assured by the home Club that at least one dozen regulation reserve balls are immediately available for use if required;

(e) Have in his possession at least two alternate balls and shall require replenishment of such supply of alternate balls as needed throughout the game. Such alternate balls shall be put in play when:

    (1) A ball has been batted out of the playing field or into the spectator area;

    (2) A ball has become discolored or unfit for further use;

    (3) The pitcher requests such alternate ball.

Rule 4.01(e) Comment: The umpire shall not give an alternate ball to the pitcher until play has ended and the previously used ball is dead. After a thrown or batted ball goes out of the playing field, play shall not be resumed with an alternate ball until the runners have reached the bases to which they are entitled. After a home run is hit out of the playing grounds, the umpire shall not deliver a new ball to the pitcher or the catcher until the batter hitting the home run has crossed the plate.

(f) Ensure that an official rosin bag is placed on the ground behind the pitcher's plate prior to the start of each game.

(g) The umpire-in-chief shall order the playing field lights turned on whenever in his opinion darkness makes further play in daylight hazardous.

4.02 Field Manager

(a) The Club shall designate the manager to the Office of the Commissioner or the umpire-in-chief not less than thirty minutes before the scheduled starting time of the game.

(b) The manager may advise the umpire-in-chief that he has delegated specific duties prescribed by the rules to a player or coach, and any action of such designated representative shall be official. The manager shall always be responsible for his team's conduct, observance of the official rules, and deference to the umpires.

(c) If a manager leaves the field, he shall designate a player or coach as his substitute, and such substitute manager shall have the duties, rights and responsibilities of the manager. If the manager fails or refuses to designate his substitute before leaving, the umpire-in-chief shall designate a team member as substitute manager.

4.03 Exchange of Lineup Cards

Unless the home Club shall have given previous notice that the game has been postponed or will be delayed in starting, the umpire, or umpires, shall enter the playing field five minutes before the hour set for the game to begin and proceed directly to home base where they shall be met by the managers of the opposing teams. In sequence:

(a) First, the home manager, or his designee, shall give his batting order to the umpire-in-chief, in duplicate.

(b) Next, the visiting manager, or his designee, shall give his batting order to the umpire-in-chief, in duplicate.

(c) As a courtesy, each lineup card presented to the umpire-in-chief should list the fielding positions to be played by each player in the batting order. If a designated hitter is to be used, the lineup card shall designate which hitter is to be the designated hitter. *See* Rule 5.11(a). As a courtesy, potential substitute players should also be listed, but the failure to list a potential substitute player shall not make such potential substitute player ineligible to enter the game.

In accordance with Major League Rule 2(b)(2), each Major League Club must designate on its lineup card in advance of that game each player eligible to play in the game as a pitcher, a position player, or a "Two-Way Player", as follows:

(1) From Opening Day through August 31 of the championship season and during postseason games, Major League Clubs may designate a maximum of 13 pitchers for a game.

(2) From September 1 through the end of the championship season (including any tiebreaker games), Major League Clubs may designate a maximum of 14 pitchers for a game.

(3) Players who qualify as "Two-Way Players" under Major League Rule 2(b)(2) may appear as pitchers during a game without counting toward a Club's pitcher limitations.

(4) No player on the lineup card other than those designated as Two-Way players or pitchers by the Club may appear in a championship season or postseason game as a pitcher, except that any player may appear as a pitcher (A) following the 9th inning of an extra inning game, (B) in any game in which his team is losing by equal to or more than 8 runs, or (C) in any game in which his team is winning by equal to or more than 10 runs in the 9th inning when the player enters as a pitcher; provided, however, that any player added to the Active List as a 27th Player prior to September 1 shall not count toward the maximum of 13 pitchers.

(d) The umpire-in-chief shall make certain that the original and copies of the respective batting orders are identical, and then tender a copy of each batting order to the opposing manager. The copy retained by the umpire shall be the official batting order. The tender of the batting order by the umpire shall establish the batting orders. Thereafter, no substitutions shall be made by either manager, except as provided in the rules.

(e) As soon as the home team's batting order is handed to the umpire-in-chief the umpires are in charge of the playing field and from that moment the umpire-in-chief shall have sole authority to determine when a game shall be called, suspended or resumed on account of weather or the condition of the playing field. The umpire-in-chief shall not call the game until at least 30 minutes after he has suspended play. The umpire-in-chief may continue the suspension so long as he believes there is any chance to resume play. Nothing in this Rule is intended to affect a Club's ability to suspend or resume any game pursuant to a policy governing severe weather, significant weather threats, and lightning safety that has been filed with the league office prior to the championship season.

Rule 4.03 Comment: Obvious errors in the batting order, which are noticed by the umpire-in-chief before he calls "Play" for the start of the game, should be called to the attention of the manager or captain of the team in error, so the correction can be made before the game starts. For example, if a manager has inadvertently listed only eight men in the batting order, or has listed two players with the same last name but without an identifying initial and the errors are noticed by the umpire before he calls "play," he shall cause such error or errors to be corrected before he calls "play" to start the game. Teams should not be "trapped" later by some mistake that obviously was inadvertent and which can be corrected before the game starts.

The umpire-in-chief shall at all times try to complete a game. His authority to resume play following one or more suspensions of as much as 30 minutes each shall be absolute and he shall terminate a game only when there appears to be no possibility of completing it.

The Major Leagues have determined that Rule 4.03(e) does not apply to any Wild Card, Division Series, League Championship Series or World Series games or for any additional Major League championship season game played to break a tie.

4.04 Weather and Field Conditions

(a) The home team shall be the sole judge as to whether a game shall not be started because of unsuitable weather conditions or the unfit condition of the playing field, except for the second game of a conventional or split doubleheader. Nothing in this Rule is intended to affect a Club's ability to suspend or resume any game pursuant to a policy governing severe weather, significant weather threats, and lightning safety that has been filed with the league office prior to the championship season.

EXCEPTION: The Office of the Commissioner may suspend the application of this rule as to a League or Leagues during the closing weeks of the championship season in order to assure that the championship is decided each year on its merits. When the postponement of, and possible failure to play, a game in the final series of a championship season between any two teams might affect the final standing of any Club in the league, the Office of the Commissioner, on appeal from any league Club, may assume the authority granted the home team by this rule.

(b) The umpire-in-chief of the first game shall be the sole judge as to whether the second game of a conventional or split doubleheader shall not be started because of unsuitable weather conditions or the unfit condition of the playing field.

(c) A postponed game shall be a "No Game" and shall be treated in the same manner as a game called before it has become a regulation game within the meaning of Rule 7.01(e).

4.05 Special Ground Rules

The manager of the home team shall present to the umpire-in-chief and the opposing manager any ground rules he thinks necessary covering the overflow of spectators upon the playing field, batted or thrown balls into such overflow, or any other contingencies. If these rules are acceptable to the opposing manager they shall be legal. If these rules are unacceptable to the opposing manager, the umpire-in-chief shall make and enforce any special ground rules he thinks are made necessary by ground conditions, which shall not conflict with the official playing rules.

4.06 No Fraternization

Players in uniform shall not address or mingle with spectators, nor sit in the stands before, during, or after a game. No manager, coach or player shall address any spectator before or during a game. Players of opposing teams shall not fraternize at any time while in uniform.

4.07 Security

(a) No person shall be allowed on the playing field during a game except players and coaches in uniform, managers, news photographers authorized by the home team, umpires, officers of the law in uniform and watchmen or other employees of the home Club.

(b) The home team shall provide police protection sufficient to preserve order. If a person, or persons, enter the playing field during a game and interfere in any way with the play, the visiting team may refuse to play until the field is cleared.

PENALTY: If the field is not cleared in a reasonable length of time, which shall in no case be less than 15 minutes after the visiting team's refusal to play, the umpire-in-chief may forfeit the game to the visiting team.

4.08 Doubleheaders

(a) (1) Only two championship games shall be played on one date. Completion of a suspended game shall not violate this rule, except for games in the Minor Leagues. *See* Rule 7.02(b) Comment.

(2) If two games are scheduled to be played for one admission on one date, the first game shall be the regularly scheduled game for that date.

(b) After the start of the first game of a conventional or split doubleheader, that game shall be completed before the second game of the doubleheader shall begin.

(c) The second game of a doubleheader shall start thirty minutes after the first game is completed, unless a longer interval (not to exceed forty-five minutes) is declared by the umpire-in-chief and announced to the opposing managers at the end of the first game.

EXCEPTION: If the Office of the Commissioner has approved a request of the home Club for a longer interval between games for some special event, the umpire-in-chief shall declare such longer interval and announce it to the opposing managers. The umpire-in-chief of the first game shall be the timekeeper controlling the interval between games.

(d) The umpire shall start the second game of a doubleheader, if at all possible, and play shall continue as long as ground conditions, local time restrictions, or weather permit.

(e) When a regularly scheduled doubleheader is delayed in starting for any cause, any game that is started is the first game of the doubleheader.

(f) When a rescheduled game is part of a doubleheader the rescheduled game shall be the second game, and the first game shall be the regularly scheduled game for that date.

(g) Between games of a doubleheader, or whenever a game is suspended because of the unfitness of the playing field, the umpire-in-chief shall have control of ground-keepers and assistants for the purpose of making the playing field fit for play.

PENALTY: For violation, the umpire-in-chief may forfeit the game to the visiting team.

5.00–PLAYING THE GAME

5.01 Starting the Game ("Play Ball!")

(a) At the time set for beginning the game the players of the home team shall take their defensive positions, the first batter of the visiting team shall take his position in the batter's box, the umpire-in-chief shall call "Play," and the game shall start.

(b) After the umpire calls "Play" the ball is alive and in play and remains alive and in play until for legal cause, or at the umpire's call of "Time" suspending play, the ball becomes dead.

(c) The pitcher shall deliver the pitch to the batter who may elect to strike the ball, or who may not offer at it, as he chooses.

5.02 Fielding Positions

When the ball is put in play at the start of, or during a game, all fielders other than the catcher shall be on fair territory.

(a) The catcher shall station himself directly back of the plate. He may leave his position at any time to catch a pitch or make a play except that when the batter is being given an intentional base on balls, the catcher must stand with both feet within the lines of the catcher's box until the ball leaves the pitcher's hand.

PENALTY: Balk.

(b) The pitcher, while in the act of delivering the ball to the batter, shall take his legal position;

(c) **Infielder Positioning**

Any fielder other than the pitcher and the catcher may station himself anywhere in fair territory, except as described below:

(i) At the time the pitcher is on the rubber and begins the natural movement associated with the delivery of the ball to the batter, the defensive team must have a minimum of four players (in addition to the pitcher and the catcher) with both feet completely in front of the outer boundary of the infield dirt;

18

Rule 5.02(c)

(ii) at the time the pitcher releases the ball for delivery to the batter, the defensive team must have a minimum of four players (in addition to the pitcher and the catcher) with both feet completely in front of the outer boundary of the infield dirt, at least two of which must be positioned with both feet entirely on each side of second base; and

(iii) from the time the pitcher releases the ball to deliver the first pitch to the first batter of a half inning, the two infielders on each side of second base may not switch sides or move to a position other than their side of the infield for the entirety of that inning. Notwithstanding the foregoing, any infielder may switch sides, or move to any other position at the time of a substitution for one of the defensive players (other than a pitching change that substitutes the pitcher for a player not already in the game). Any player who legally replaces an infielder during an inning also may not switch sides or move to a position other than their side of the infield from the time the pitcher releases the ball to deliver the first pitch following the substitution to the end of that half inning (except upon the occurrence of a subsequent substitution during that half inning).

Rule 5.02(c) Comment. Umpires should bear in mind that the purpose of the Infielder Positioning rule is to prevent the defense from having more than two infielders on either side of second base in an effort to anticipate where the batter will hit the ball prior to delivery of the pitch. If, in the judgment of the umpire, any fielder attempts to circumvent the purposes of this Rule 5.02(c), the umpire shall assess the penalty described below.

PENALTY: If the defensive team violates Rule 5.02(c), the pitch shall be called a "ball" and the ball is dead, unless the batter reaches first base on a hit, an error, a base on balls, a hit batter, or otherwise, and all other runners advance at least one base, in which case the play proceeds without reference to the violation. If any other play follows the violation (e.g., sacrifice fly, sacrifice bunt, etc.), the manager of the offense may advise the plate umpire that he elects to decline the penalty and accept the play. Such election shall be made immediately at the end of the play.

5.03 Base Coaches

(a) The team at bat shall station two base coaches on the field during its time at bat, one near first base and one near third base.

(b) Base coaches shall be limited to two in number and shall be in team uniform.

(c) Base coaches must remain within the coach's box consistent with this Rule, except that a coach who has a play at his base may leave the coach's box to signal the player to slide, advance or return to a base if the coach does not interfere with the play in any manner. Other than exchanging equipment, all base coaches shall refrain from physically touching base runners, especially when signs are being given.

PENALTY: If a coach has positioned himself closer to home plate than the coach's box or closer to fair territory than the coach's box before a batted ball passes the coach, the umpire shall, upon complaint by the opposing manager, strictly enforce the rule. The umpire shall warn the coach and instruct him to return to the box. If the coach does not return to the box he shall be removed from the game. In addition, coaches who violate this Rule may be subject to discipline by the Office of the Commissioner.

5.04 Batting

(a) **Batting Order**

(1) Each player of the offensive team shall bat in the order that his name appears in his team's batting order.

(2) The batting order shall be followed throughout the game unless a player is substituted for another. In that case the substitute shall take the place of the replaced player in the batting order.

(3) The first batter in each inning after the first inning shall be the player whose name follows that of the last player

who legally completed his time at bat in the preceding inning.

(b) **The Batter's Box**

    (1) The batter shall take his position in the batter's box promptly when it is his time at bat.

    (2) The batter shall not leave his position in the batter's box after the pitcher comes to Set Position, or starts his windup.

PENALTY: If the pitcher pitches, the umpire shall call "Ball" or "Strike," as the case may be.

Rule 5.04(b)(2) Comment: The batter leaves the batter's box at the risk of having a strike delivered and called, unless he requests the umpire to call "Time." The batter is not at liberty to step in and out of the batter's box at will.

Once a batter has taken his position in the batter's box, he shall not be permitted to step out of the batter's box in order to use the rosin or the pine tar rag, unless there is a delay in the game action or, in the judgment of the umpires, weather conditions warrant an exception.

Umpires will not call "Time" at the request of the batter or any member of his team once the pitcher has started his windup or has come to a set position even though the batter claims "dust in his eyes," "steamed glasses," "didn't get the sign" or for any other cause.

Umpires may grant a hitter's request for "Time" once he is in the batter's box, but the umpire should eliminate hitters walking out of the batter's box without reason. If umpires are not lenient, batters will understand that they are in the batter's box and they must remain there until the ball is pitched. *See* Rule 5.04(b)(4).

If pitcher delays once the batter is in his box and the umpire feels that the delay is not justified he may allow the batter to step out of the box momentarily.

If after the pitcher starts his windup or comes to a "set position" with a runner on, he does not go through with his pitch because the batter has inadvertently caused the pitcher to interrupt his delivery, it shall not be called a balk. Both the pitcher and batter have violated a rule and the umpire shall call time and both the batter and pitcher start over from "scratch."

The following paragraph is additional material for Rule 5.04(b)(2) Comment, for Minor League play:

If after the pitcher starts his windup or comes to a "set position" with a runner on, he does not go through with his pitch because the batter has stepped out of the box, the umpire shall not call a balk. Such action by the batter shall be treated as a violation of the Batter's Box Rule and shall subject a batter to the penalties set forth in Rule 5.04(b)(4)(A).

(3) If the batter refuses to take his position in the batter's box during his time at bat, the umpire shall call a strike on the batter. The ball is dead, and no runners may advance. After the penalty, the batter may take his proper position and the regular ball and strike count shall continue. If the batter does not take his proper position before three strikes have been called, the batter shall be declared out.

Rule 5.04(b)(3) Comment: The umpire shall give the batter a reasonable opportunity to take his proper position in the batter's box after the umpire has called a strike pursuant to Rule 5.04(b)(3) and before the umpire calls a successive strike pursuant to Rule 5.04(b)(3).

(4) **The Batter's Box Rule**

(A) The batter shall keep at least one foot in the batter's box throughout the batter's time at bat, unless one of the following exceptions applies, in which case the batter may leave the batter's box but not the dirt area surrounding home plate:

(i) The batter swings at a pitch;

(ii) An attempted check swing is appealed to a base umpire;

(iii) The batter is forced off balance or out of the batter's box by a pitch;

(iv)   A member of either team requests and is granted "Time";

(v)   A defensive player attempts a play on a runner at any base;

(vi)   The batter feints a bunt;

(vii) A wild pitch or passed ball occurs;

(viii) The pitcher leaves the dirt area of the pitching mound after receiving the ball; or

(ix)   The catcher leaves the catcher's box to give defensive signals.

If the batter intentionally leaves the batter's box and delays play, and none of the exceptions listed in Rule 5.04(b)(4)(A) (i) through (ix) applies, the umpire shall issue a warning to the batter for the batter's first violation of this Rule in a game. For a batter's second or subsequent violations of this Rule in a game, the Office of the Commissioner may issue an appropriate discipline. In Minor League play, for a batter's second or subsequent violations of this Rule in a game, the umpire shall award a strike without the pitcher having to deliver the pitch. The ball is dead, and no runners may advance.

(B)   The batter may leave the batter's box and the dirt area surrounding home plate when "Time" is called for the purpose or as a result of

(i) an injury or potential injury;

(ii) making a substitution; or

(iii) a conference by either team.

Rule 5.04(b)(4)(B) Comment: Umpires shall encourage the on-deck batter to take a position in the batter's box quickly after the previous batter reaches base or is put out.

(5)   The batter's legal position shall be with both feet within the batter's box.

APPROVED RULING: The lines defining the box are within the batter's box.

(c) Completing Time at Bat

A batter has legally completed his time at bat when he is put out or becomes a runner.

5.05 When the Batter Becomes a Runner

(a) The batter becomes a runner when:

(1) He hits a fair ball;

Rule 5.05(a) Comment: If the batter hits a pitch that touches the ground first, the ensuing action shall be the same as if he hit the ball in flight.

(2) The third strike called by the umpire is not caught, providing (1) first base is unoccupied, or (2) first base is occupied with two out;

Rule 5.05(a)(2) Comment: A batter who does not realize his situation on a third strike not caught, and who is not in the process of running to first base, shall be declared out once he leaves the dirt circle surrounding home plate.

(3) If the pitch touches the ground and bounces through the strike zone it is a "ball." If such a pitch touches the batter, he shall be awarded first base. If the batter swings at such a pitch after two strikes, the ball cannot be caught, for the purposes of Rule 5.05(b) and 5.09(a)(3).

(4) A fair ball, after having passed a fielder other than the pitcher, or after having been touched by a fielder, including the pitcher, shall touch an umpire or runner on fair territory;

(5) A fair ball passes over a fence or into the stands at a distance from home base of 250 feet or more. Such hit entitles the batter to a home run when he shall have touched all bases legally. A fair fly ball that passes out of the playing field at a point less than 250 feet from home base shall entitle the batter to advance to second base only;

(6) A fair ball, after touching the ground, bounds into the stands, or passes through, over or under a fence, or through

24

or under a scoreboard, or through or under shrubbery, or vines on the fence, in which case the batter and the runners shall be entitled to advance two bases;

(7) Any fair ball which, either before or after touching the ground, passes through or under a fence, or through or under a scoreboard, or through any opening in the fence or scoreboard, or through or under shrubbery, or vines on the fence, or which sticks in a fence or scoreboard, in which case the batter and the runners shall be entitled to two bases;

(8) Any bounding fair ball is deflected by the fielder into the stands, or over or under a fence on fair or foul territory, in which case the batter and all runners shall be entitled to advance two bases;

(9) Any fair fly ball is deflected by the fielder into the stands, or over the fence into foul territory, in which case the batter shall be entitled to advance to second base; but if deflected into the stands or over the fence in fair territory, the batter shall be entitled to a home run. However, should such a fair fly be deflected at a point less than 250 feet from home plate, the batter shall be entitled to two bases only.

(b) The batter becomes a runner and is entitled to first base without liability to be put out (provided he advances to and touches first base) when:

(1) Four "balls" have been called by the umpire;

Rule 5.05(b)(1) Comment: A batter who is entitled to first base because of a base on balls, including an award of first base to a batter by an umpire following a signal from a manager, must go to first base and touch the base before other base runners are forced to advance. This applies when bases are full and applies when a substitute runner is put into the game.

If, in advancing, the base runner thinks there is a play and he slides past the base before or after touching it he may be put out by the fielder tagging him. If he fails to touch the base to which he is entitled and attempts to advance beyond that base he may be put out by tagging him or the base he missed.

(2) He is touched by a pitched ball which he is not attempting to hit unless (A) The ball is in the strike zone when it touches the batter, or (B) The batter makes no attempt to avoid being touched by the ball;

If the ball is in the strike zone when it touches the batter, it shall be called a strike, whether or not the batter tries to avoid the ball. If the ball is outside the strike zone when it touches the batter, it shall be called a ball if he makes no attempt to avoid being touched.

APPROVED RULING: When the batter is touched by a pitched ball which does not entitle him to first base, the ball is dead and no runner may advance.

Rule 5.05(b)(2) Comment: A batter shall not be considered touched by a pitched ball if the ball only touches any jewelry being worn by a player (e.g., necklaces, bracelets, etc.).

(3) The catcher or any fielder interferes with him. If a play follows the interference, the manager of the offense may advise the plate umpire that he elects to decline the interference penalty and accept the play. Such election shall be made immediately at the end of the play. However, if the batter reaches first base on a hit, an error, a base on balls, a hit batsman, or otherwise, and all other runners advance at least one base, the play proceeds without reference to the interference.

Rule 5.05(b)(3) Comment: If catcher's interference is called with a play in progress the umpire will allow the play to continue because the manager may elect to take the play. If the batter-runner missed first base, or a runner misses his next base, he shall be considered as having reached the base, as stated in Note of Rule 5.06(b)(3)(D).

Examples of plays the manager might elect to take:

1. Runner on third, one out, batter hits fly ball to the outfield on which the runner scores but catcher's interference was called. The offensive manager may elect to take the run and have batter called out or have runner remain at third and batter awarded first base.

2. Runner on second base. Catcher interferes with batter as he bunts ball fairly sending runner to third base. The manager may rather have runner on third base with an out on the play than have runners on second and first.

If a runner is trying to score by a steal or squeeze from third base, note the additional penalty set forth in Rule 6.01(g).

If the catcher interferes with the batter before the pitcher delivers the ball, it shall not be considered interference on the batter under Rule 5.05(b)(3). In such cases, the umpire shall call "Time" and the pitcher and batter start over from "scratch."

(4) A fair ball touches an umpire or a runner on fair territory before touching a fielder.

If a fair ball touches an umpire after having passed a fielder other than the pitcher, or having touched a fielder, including the pitcher, the ball is in play.

5.06 Running the Bases

(a) Occupying the Base

(1) A runner acquires the right to an unoccupied base when he touches it before he is out. He is then entitled to it until he is put out, or forced to vacate it for another runner legally entitled to that base.

Rule 5.06(a)/5.06(c) Comment: If a runner legally acquires title to a base, and the pitcher assumes his pitching position, the runner may not return to a previously occupied base.

(2) Two runners may not occupy a base, but if, while the ball is alive, two runners are touching a base, the following runner shall be out when tagged and the preceding runner is entitled to the base, unless Rule 5.06(b)(2) applies.

(b) Advancing Bases

(1) In advancing, a runner shall touch first, second, third and home base in order. If forced to return, he shall retouch all bases in reverse order, unless the ball is dead under any

provision of Rule 5.06(c). In such cases, the runner may go directly to his original base.

(2) If a runner is forced to advance by reason of the batter becoming a runner and two runners are touching a base to which the following runner is forced, the following runner is entitled to the base and the preceding runner shall be out when tagged or when a fielder possesses the ball and touches the base to which such preceding runner is forced.

(3) Each runner, other than the batter, may without liability to be put out, advance one base when:

(A) There is a balk;

(B) The batter's advance without liability to be put out forces the runner to vacate his base, or when the batter hits a fair ball that touches another runner or the umpire before such ball has been touched by, or has passed a fielder, if the runner is forced to advance;

Rule 5.06(b)(3)(B) Comment: A runner forced to advance without liability to be put out may advance past the base to which he is entitled only at his peril. If such a runner, forced to advance, is put out for the third out before a preceding runner, also forced to advance, touches home plate, the run shall score.

Play. Two out, bases full, batter walks but runner from second is overzealous and runs past third base toward home and is tagged out on a throw by the catcher. Even though two are out, the run would score on the theory that the run was forced home by the base on balls and that all the runners needed to do was proceed and touch the next base.

(C) A fielder, after catching a fly ball, steps or falls into any out-of-play area;

Rule 5.06(b)(3)(C) Comment: If a fielder, after having made a legal catch, should step or fall into any out-of-play area, the ball is dead and each runner shall advance one base, without liability to be put out, from his last legally touched base at the time the fielder entered such out-of-play area.

(D) While he is attempting to steal a base, the batter is interfered with by the catcher or any other fielder.

NOTE: When a runner is entitled to a base without liability to be put out, while the ball is in play, or under any rule in which the ball is in play after the runner reaches the base to which he is entitled, and the runner fails to touch the base to which he is entitled before attempting to advance to the next base, the runner shall forfeit his exemption from liability to be put out, and he may be put out by tagging the base or by tagging the runner before he returns to the missed base;

(E) A fielder deliberately touches a pitched ball with his cap, mask or any part of his uniform detached from its proper place on his person. The ball is in play, and the award is made from the position of the runner at the time the ball was touched.

(4) Each runner including the batter-runner may, without liability to be put out, advance:

(A) To home base, scoring a run, if a fair ball goes out of the playing field in flight and he touched all bases legally; or if a fair ball which, in the umpire's judgment, would have gone out of the playing field in flight, is deflected by the act of a fielder in throwing his glove, cap, or any article of his apparel;

(B) Three bases, if a fielder deliberately touches a fair ball with his cap, mask or any part of his uniform detached from its proper place on his person. The ball is in play and the batter may advance to home base at his peril;

(C) Three bases, if a fielder deliberately throws his glove at and touches a fair ball. The ball is in play and the batter may advance to home base at his peril;

(D) Two bases, if a fielder deliberately touches a thrown ball with his cap, mask or any part of his uniform detached from its proper place on his person. The ball is in play;

(E) Two bases, if a fielder deliberately throws his glove at and touches a thrown ball. The ball is in play;

Rule 5.06(b)(4)(B) through (E) Comment: In applying (B-C-D-E) the umpire must rule that the thrown glove or detached cap or mask has touched the ball. There is no penalty if the ball is not touched.

Under (C-E) this penalty shall not be invoked against a fielder whose glove is carried off his hand by the force of a batted or thrown ball, or when his glove flies off his hand as he makes an obvious effort to make a legitimate catch.

(F) Two bases, if a fair ball bounces or is deflected into the stands outside the first or third base foul lines; or if it goes through or under a field fence, or through or under a scoreboard, or through or under shrubbery or vines on the fence; or if it sticks in such fence, scoreboard, shrubbery or vines;

(G) Two bases when, with no spectators on the playing field, a thrown ball goes into the stands, or into a bench (whether or not the ball rebounds into the field), or over or under or through a field fence, or on a slanting part of the screen above the backstop, or remains in the meshes of a wire screen protecting spectators. The ball is dead. When such wild throw is the first play by an infielder, the umpire, in awarding such bases, shall be governed by the position of the runners at the time the ball was pitched; in all other cases the umpire shall be governed by the position of the runners at the time the wild throw was made;

APPROVED RULING: If all runners, including the batter-runner, have advanced at least one base when an infielder makes a wild throw on the first play after the pitch, the award shall be governed by the position of the runners when the wild throw was made.

Rule 5.06(b)(4)(G) Comment: In certain circumstances it is impossible to award a runner two bases. Example: Runner on first. Batter hits fly to short right. Runner holds up between first and second and batter comes around first and pulls up behind him. Ball falls safely. Outfielder, in throwing to first, throws ball into stands.

APPROVED RULING: Since no runner, when the ball is dead, may advance beyond the base to which he is entitled, the runner originally on first base goes to third base and the batter is held at second base.

The term "when the wild throw was made" means when the throw actually left the player's hand and not when the thrown ball hit the ground, passes a receiving fielder or goes out of play into the stands.

The position of the batter-runner at the time the wild throw left the thrower's hand is the key in deciding the award of bases. If the batter-runner has not reached first base, the award is two bases at the time the pitch was made for all runners. The decision as to whether the batter-runner has reached first base before the throw is a judgment call.

If an unusual play arises where a first throw by an infielder goes into stands or dugout but the batter did not become a runner (such as catcher throwing ball into stands in attempt to get runner from third trying to score on passed ball or wild pitch) award of two bases shall be from the position of the runners at the time of the throw. (For the purpose of Rule 5.06(b)(4)(G) a catcher is considered an infielder.)

PLAY—Runner on first base, batter hits a ball to the shortstop, who throws to second base too late to get runner at second, and second baseman throws toward first base after batter has crossed first base.

RULING: Runner at second scores. (On this play, only if batter-runner is past first base when throw is made is he awarded third base.)

(H) One base, if a ball, pitched to the batter, or thrown by the pitcher from his position on the pitcher's plate to a base to catch a runner, goes into a stand or a bench, or over or through a field fence or backstop. The ball is dead;

APPROVED RULING: When a wild pitch or passed ball goes through or by the catcher, or deflects off the catcher, and goes directly into the dugout, stands, above the break, or any area where the ball is dead, the awarding of bases shall be one base. One base shall also be awarded if the pitcher while in contact with the rubber, throws to a base, and the throw goes directly into the stands or into any area where the ball is dead.

If, however, the pitched or thrown ball goes through or by the catcher or through the fielder, and remains on the playing field, and is subsequently kicked or deflected into the dugout, stands or other area where the ball is dead, the awarding of bases shall be two bases from position of runners at the time of the pitch or throw.

    (I) One base, if the batter becomes a runner on Ball Four or Strike Three, when the pitch passes the catcher and lodges in the umpire's mask or paraphernalia.

    If the batter becomes a runner on a wild pitch which entitles the runners to advance one base, the batter-runner shall be entitled to first base only.

Rule 5.06(b)(4)(I) Comment: The fact a runner is awarded a base or bases without liability to be put out does not relieve him of the responsibility to touch the base he is awarded and all intervening bases. For example: Batter hits a ground ball which an infielder throws into the stands but the batter-runner missed first base. He may be called out on appeal for missing first base after the ball is put in play even though he was "awarded" second base.

If a runner is forced to return to a base after a catch, he must retouch his original base even though, because of some ground rule or other rule, he is awarded additional bases. He may retouch while the ball is dead and the award is then made from his original base.

(c) Dead Balls

The ball becomes dead and runners advance one base, or return to their bases, without liability to be put out, when:

(1) A pitched ball touches a batter, or his clothing, while in his legal batting position; runners, if forced, advance;

(2) The plate umpire interferes with the catcher's throw attempting to prevent a stolen base or retire a runner on a pick-off play; runners may not advance.

NOTE: The interference shall be disregarded if the catcher's throw retires the runner.

While the ball is dead no player may be put out, no bases may be run and no runs may be scored, except that runners may advance one or more bases as the result of acts which occurred while the ball was alive (such as, but not limited to a balk, an overthrow, interference, or a home run or other fair ball hit out of the playing field).

Rule 5.06(c)(2) Comment: Umpire interference may also occur when an umpire interferes with a catcher returning the ball to the pitcher.

(3) A balk is committed; runners advance; (*See* Penalty 6.02(a).)

(4) A ball is illegally batted; runners return;

(5) A foul ball is not caught, in which case runners return to their bases. The umpire-in-chief shall not put the ball in play until all runners have retouched their bases;

(6) A fair ball touches a runner or an umpire on fair territory before it touches an infielder including the pitcher, or touches an umpire before it has passed an infielder other than the pitcher; runners advance, if forced.

If a fair ball goes through, or by, an infielder, no other infielder has a chance to make a play on the ball and the ball touches a runner immediately behind the infielder that the ball went through, or by, the ball is in play and the umpire shall not declare the runner out. If a fair ball touches a runner after being deflected by an infielder, the ball is in play and the umpire shall not declare the runner out;

Rule 5.06(c)(6) Comment: If a fair ball touches an umpire working in the infield after it has bounded past, or over, the pitcher, it is a dead ball. If a batted ball is deflected by a fielder in fair territory and hits a runner or an umpire while still in flight and then caught by an infielder it shall not be a catch, but the ball shall remain in play.

(7) A pitched ball lodges in the catcher's mask or paraphernalia, or in or against the umpire's body, mask or paraphernalia, and remains out of play, runners advance one base;

Rule 5.06(c)(7) Comment: If a foul tip hits the umpire and is caught by a fielder on the rebound, the ball is "dead" and the batsman cannot be called out. The same shall apply where such foul tip lodges in the umpire's mask or other paraphernalia.

If a third strike (not a foul tip) passes the catcher and hits an umpire, the ball is in play. If such ball rebounds and is caught by a fielder before it touches the ground, the batsman is not out on such a catch, but the ball remains in play and the batsman may be retired at first base, or touched with the ball for the out.

If a pitched ball lodges in the umpire's or catcher's mask or paraphernalia, and remains out of play, on the third strike or fourth ball, then the batter is entitled to first base and all runners advance one base. If the count on the batter is less than three balls, runners advance one base.

If a ball is intentionally placed inside a player's uniform (e.g., a pants pocket) for the purpose of deceiving a base runner, the umpire shall call "Time." The umpire will place all runners at least one base (or more if warranted, in the umpire's judgment, in order to nullify the action of the ball being put out of play), from the base they originally occupied.

(8) Any legal pitch touches a runner trying to score; runners advance.

5.07 Pitching

(a) Legal Pitching Delivery

There are two legal pitching positions, the Windup Position and the Set Position, and either position may be used at any time.

Pitchers shall take signs from the catcher while in contact with the pitcher's plate.

Rule 5.07(a) Comment: Pitchers may disengage the rubber after taking their signs but may not step quickly onto the rubber and pitch. This may be judged a quick pitch by the umpire. When the pitcher disengages the rubber, he must drop his hands to his sides.

Pitchers will not be allowed to disengage the rubber after taking each sign.

The pitcher may not take a second step toward home plate with either foot or otherwise reset his pivot foot in his delivery of the pitch. If there is a runner, or runners, on base it is a balk under Rule 6.02(a); if the bases are unoccupied it should be treated as an illegal pitch under Rule 6.02(b).

(1) The Windup Position

The pitcher shall stand facing the batter, his pivot foot in contact with the pitcher's plate and the other foot free. From this position any natural movement associated with his delivery of the ball to the batter commits him to the pitch without interruption or alteration. He shall not raise either foot from the ground, except that in his actual delivery of the ball to the batter, he may take one step backward, and one step forward with his free foot.

When a pitcher holds the ball with both hands in front of his body, with his pivot foot in contact with the pitcher's plate and his other foot free, he will be considered in the Windup Position.

Rule 5.07(a)(1) Comment: In the Windup Position, a pitcher is permitted to have his "free" foot on the rubber, in front of the rubber, behind the rubber or off the side of the rubber.

From the Windup Position, the pitcher may:

(A) deliver the ball to the batter, or

(B) step and throw to a base in an attempt to pick-off a runner, or

(C) disengage the rubber (if he does he must drop his hand to his sides).

In disengaging the rubber the pitcher must step off with his pivot foot and not his free foot first. He may not go into a set or stretch position—if he does it is a balk.

(2) The Set Position

Set Position shall be indicated by the pitcher when he stands facing the batter with his pivot foot in contact with, and his other foot in front of, the pitcher's plate, holding the ball in both hands in front of his body and coming to a complete stop. From such Set Position he may deliver the ball to the batter, throw to a base or step backward off the pitcher's plate with his pivot foot. Before assuming Set Position, the pitcher may elect to make any natural preliminary motion such as that known as "the stretch." But if he so elects, he shall come to Set Position before delivering the ball to the batter. After assuming Set Position, any natural motion associated with his delivery of the ball to the batter commits him to the pitch without alteration or interruption.

Preparatory to coming to a set position, the pitcher shall have one hand on his side; from this position he shall go to his set position as defined in Rule 5.07(a)(2) without interruption and in one continuous motion.

The pitcher, following his stretch, must (a) hold the ball in both hands in front of his body and (b) come to a complete stop. This must be enforced. Umpires should watch this closely. Pitchers are constantly attempting to "beat the rule" in their efforts to hold runners on bases and in cases where the pitcher fails to make a complete "stop" called for in the rules, the umpire should immediately call a "Balk."

Rule 5.07(a)(2) Comment: With no runners on base, the pitcher is not required to come to a complete stop when using the Set Position. If, however, in the umpire's judgment, a pitcher delivers the ball in a deliberate effort to catch the batter off guard, this delivery shall be deemed a quick pitch, for which the penalty is a ball. *See* Rule 6.02(a)(5) Comment.

With a runner or runners on base, a pitcher will be presumed to be pitching from the Set Position if he stands with his pivot foot in contact with and parallel to the pitcher's plate, and his other foot in front of the pitcher's plate, unless he notifies the umpire that he will be pitching from the Windup Position under such circumstances prior to the beginning of an at-bat. A pitcher will be permitted to notify the umpire that he is pitching from the Windup Position within an at-bat only in the event of (i) a substitution by the offensive team; or (ii) immediately upon the advancement of one or more runners (i.e., after one or more base runners advance but before the delivery of the next pitch).

(b) **Warm-Up Pitches**

When a pitcher takes his position at the beginning of each inning, or when he relieves another pitcher, he shall be permitted to pitch preparatory pitches to his catcher during which play shall be suspended. A league by its own action may limit the number of preparatory pitches and/or may limit the amount of time such preparatory pitches may consume. If a sudden emergency causes a pitcher to be summoned into the game without any opportunity to warm up, the umpire-in-chief shall allow him as many pitches as the umpire deems necessary.

(c) **Pitcher Delays**

When the bases are unoccupied, the pitcher shall deliver the ball to the batter within 12 seconds after he receives the ball. Each time the pitcher delays the game by violating this rule, the umpire shall call "Ball."

The 12-second timing starts when the pitcher is in possession of the ball and the batter is in the box, alert to the pitcher. The timing stops when the pitcher releases the ball.

The intent of this rule is to avoid unnecessary delays. The umpire shall insist that the catcher return the ball promptly to the pitcher, and that the pitcher take his position on the rubber promptly. Obvious delay by the pitcher should instantly be penalized by the umpire.

(d) Throwing to the Bases

At any time during the pitcher's preliminary movements and until his natural pitching motion commits him to the pitch, he may throw to any base provided he steps directly toward such base before making the throw.

Rule 5.07(d) Comment: The pitcher shall step "ahead of the throw." A snap throw followed by the step directly toward the base is a balk.

(e) Effect of Removing Pivot Foot From Plate

If the pitcher removes his pivot foot from contact with the pitcher's plate by stepping backward with that foot, he thereby becomes an infielder and if he makes a wild throw from that position, it shall be considered the same as a wild throw by any other infielder.

Rule 5.07(e) Comment: The pitcher, while off the rubber, may throw to any base. If he makes a wild throw, such throw is the throw of an infielder and what follows is governed by the rules covering a ball thrown by a fielder.

(f) Ambidextrous Pitchers

A pitcher must indicate visually to the umpire-in-chief, the batter and any runners the hand with which he intends to pitch, which may be done by wearing his glove on the other hand while touching the pitcher's plate. The pitcher is not permitted to pitch with the other hand until the batter is retired, the batter becomes a runner, the inning ends, the batter is substituted for by a pinch-hitter or the pitcher incurs an injury. In the event a pitcher switches pitching hands during an at-bat because he has suffered an injury, the pitcher may not, for the remainder of the game, pitch with the hand from which he has switched. The pitcher shall not be given the opportunity to throw any preparatory pitches after switching pitching hands. Any change of pitching hands must be indicated clearly to the umpire-in-chief.

5.08 How a Team Scores

(a) One run shall be scored each time a runner legally advances to and touches first, second, third and home base before three men are put out to end the inning.

EXCEPTION: A run is not scored if the runner advances to home base during a play in which the third out is made (1) by the batter-runner before he touches first base; (2) by any runner being forced out; or (3) by a preceding runner who is declared out because he failed to touch one of the bases.

Rule 5.08(a) Comment: A run legally scored cannot be nullified by subsequent action of the runner, such as but not limited to an effort to return to third base in the belief that he had left the base before a caught fly ball.

(b) When the winning run is scored in the last half-inning of a regulation game, or in the last half of an extra inning, as the result of a base on balls, hit batter or any other play with the bases full which forces the batter and all other runners to advance without liability of being put out, the umpire shall not declare the game ended until the runner forced to advance from third has touched home base and the batter-runner has touched first base.

Rule 5.08(b) Comment: An exception will be if fans rush onto the field and physically prevent the runner from touching home plate or the batter from touching first base. In such cases, the umpires shall award the runner the base because of the obstruction by the fans.

PENALTY: If the runner on third refuses to advance to and touch home base in a reasonable time, the umpire shall disallow the run, call out the offending player and order the game resumed. If, with two out, the batter-runner refuses to advance to and touch first base, the umpire shall disallow the run, call out the offending player, and order the game resumed. If, before two are out, the batter-runner refuses to advance to and touch first base, the run shall count, but the offending player shall be called out.

Rule 5.08 Comment:

APPROVED RULING: No run shall score during a play in which the third out is made by the batter-runner before he touches first base. Example: One out, Jones on second, Smith on first. The batter, Brown, hits safely. Jones scores. Smith is out on the throw to the plate. Two outs. But Brown missed first base. The ball is thrown to first, an appeal is made, and Brown is out. Three outs. Since Jones crossed the plate during a play in which the third out was made by the batter-runner before he touched first base, Jones' run does not count.

APPROVED RULING: Following runners are not affected by an act of a preceding runner unless two are out.

EXAMPLE: One out, Jones on second, Smith on first, and batter, Brown, hits home run inside the park. Jones fails to touch third on his way to the plate. Smith and Brown score. The defense holds the ball on third, appeals to umpire, and Jones is out. Smith's and Brown's runs count.

APPROVED RULING: Two out, Jones on second, Smith on first and batter, Brown, hits home run inside the park. All three runs cross the plate. But Jones missed third base, and on appeal is declared out. Three outs. Smith's and Brown's runs are voided. No score on the play.

APPROVED RULING: One out, Jones on third, Smith on second. Batter Brown flies out to center. Two out. Jones scores after catch and Smith scores on bad throw to plate. But Jones, on appeal, is adjudged to have left third before the catch and is out. Three outs. No runs.

APPROVED RULING: Two out, bases full, batter hits home run over fence. Batter, on appeal, is declared out for missing first base. Three outs. No run counts.

Here is a general statement that covers:

When a runner misses a base and a fielder holds the ball on a missed base, or on the base originally occupied by the runner if a fly ball is caught, and appeals for the umpire's decision, the runner is out when the umpire sustains the appeal; all runners may score if possible, except that with two out the runner is out at the moment he misses the bag, if an appeal is sustained as applied to the following runners.

APPROVED RULING: One out, Jones on third, Smith on first, and Brown flies out to right field. Two outs. Jones tags up and scores after the catch. Smith attempted to return to first but the right fielder's throw beat him to the base. Three outs. But Jones scored before the throw to catch Smith reached first base, hence Jones' run counts. It was not a force play.

5.09 Making an Out

(a) Retiring the Batter

A batter is out when:

(1) His fair or foul fly ball (other than a foul tip) is legally caught by a fielder;

Rule 5.09(a)(1) Comment: A fielder may reach into, but not step into, a dugout to make a catch, and if he holds the ball, the catch shall be allowed. A fielder, in order to make a catch on a foul ball nearing a dugout or other out-of-play area (such as the stands), must have one or both feet on or over the playing surface (including the lip of the dugout) and neither foot on the ground inside the dugout or in any other out-of-play area. Ball is in play, unless the fielder, after making a legal catch, steps or falls into a dugout or other out-of-play area, in which case the ball is dead. Status of runners shall be as described in Rule 5.06(b)(3)(C) Comment.

A catch is the act of a fielder in getting secure possession in his hand or glove of a ball in flight and firmly holding it; providing he does not use his cap, protector, pocket or any other part of his uniform in getting possession. It is not a catch, however, if simultaneously or immediately following his contact with the ball, he collides with a player, or with a wall, or if he falls down, and as a result of such collision or falling, drops the ball. It is not a catch if a fielder touches

41

a fly ball which then hits a member of the offensive team or an umpire and then is caught by another defensive player. In establishing the validity of the catch, the fielder shall hold the ball long enough to prove that he has complete control of the ball and that his release of the ball is voluntary and intentional. If the fielder has made the catch and drops the ball while in the act of making a throw following the catch, the ball shall be adjudged to have been caught.

Catch Comment: A catch is legal if the ball is finally held by any fielder, even though juggled, or held by another fielder before it touches the ground. Runners may leave their bases the instant the first fielder touches the ball. A fielder may reach over a fence, railing, rope or other line of demarcation to make a catch. He may jump on top of a railing, or canvas that may be in foul ground. No interference should be allowed when a fielder reaches over a fence, railing, rope or into a stand to catch a ball. He does so at his own risk.

If a fielder, attempting a catch at the edge of the dugout, is "held up" and kept from an apparent fall by a player or players of either team and the catch is made, it shall be allowed.

(2) A third strike is legally caught by the catcher;

Rule 5.09(a)(2) Comment: "Legally caught" means in the catcher's glove before the ball touches the ground. It is not legal if the ball lodges in his clothing or paraphernalia; or if it touches the umpire and is caught by the catcher on the rebound.

If a foul tip first strikes any part of the catcher's body or paraphernalia and is caught by hand or glove against his body or protector, before the ball touches the ground, it is a strike, and if third strike, batter is out.

(3) A third strike is not caught by the catcher when first base is occupied before two are out;

(4) He bunts foul on third strike;

(5) An Infield Fly is declared;

(6) He attempts to hit a third strike and the ball touches him;

(7) His fair ball touches him before touching a fielder. If the batter is in a legal position in the batter's box, *see* Rule 5.04(b)(5), and, in the umpire's judgment, there was no intention to interfere with the course of the ball, a batted ball that strikes the batter or his bat shall be ruled a foul ball;

(8) After hitting or bunting a fair ball, his bat hits the ball a second time in fair territory. The ball is dead and no runners may advance. If the batter-runner drops his bat and the ball rolls against the bat in fair territory and, in the umpire's judgment, there was no intention to interfere with the course of the ball, the ball is alive and in play. If the batter is in a legal position in the batter's box, *see* Rule 5.04(b)(5), and, in the umpire's judgment, there was no intention to interfere with the course of the ball, a batted ball that strikes the batter or his bat shall be ruled a foul ball;

Rule 5.09(a)(8) Comment: If a bat breaks and part of it is in fair territory and is hit by a batted ball or part of it hits a runner or fielder, play shall continue and no interference called. If a batted ball hits part of a broken bat in foul territory, it is a foul ball.

If a whole bat is thrown into fair or foul territory and interferes with a defensive player attempting to make a play, interference shall be called, whether intentional or not.

In cases where the batting helmet is accidentally hit with a batted ball on or over fair territory or a thrown ball, the ball remains in play the same as if it has not hit the helmet.

If a batted ball strikes a batting helmet or any other object foreign to the natural ground while on foul territory, it is a foul ball and the ball is dead.

If, in the umpire's judgment, there is intent on the part of a base runner to interfere with a batted or thrown ball by dropping the helmet or throwing it at the ball, then the runner would be out, the ball dead and runners would return to last base legally touched.

43

(9) After hitting or bunting a ball that continues to move over foul territory, he intentionally deflects the course of the ball in any manner while running to first base. The ball is dead and no runners may advance;

(10) After a third strike or after he hits a fair ball, he or first base is tagged before he touches first base;

(11) In running the last half of the distance from home base to first base, while the ball is being fielded to first base, he runs outside (to the right of) the three-foot line, or inside (to the left of) the foul line and on the infield grass, and in the umpire's judgment in so doing interferes with the fielder taking the throw at first base, in which case the ball is dead; except that he may run outside (to the right of) the three-foot line or inside (to the left of) the foul line and on the infield grass to avoid a fielder attempting to field a batted ball;

Rule 5.09(a)(11) Comment: The chalk lines marking the three-foot lane are a part of that lane and a batter-runner is required to have both feet within the three-foot lane, on the lines marking the lane, or on the dirt inside (to the left of) the foul line in running the last half of the distance from home base to first base. The umpire will determine that the batter-runner complied with Rule 5.09(a)(11) if the batter had both feet within the three-foot lane, or on the lines marking the lane, or on the dirt inside of the foul line (A) after reaching the last half of the distance from home base to first base, or (B) after the ball is released by a fielder in a throw to first base, whichever is later.

(12) An infielder intentionally drops a fair fly ball or line drive, with first, first and second, first and third, or first, second and third base occupied before two are out. The ball is dead and runner or runners shall return to their original base or bases;

APPROVED RULING: In this situation, the batter is not out if the infielder permits the ball to drop untouched to the ground, except when the Infield Fly rule applies.

(13) A preceding runner shall, in the umpire's judgment, intentionally interfere with a fielder who is attempting to catch a thrown ball or to throw a ball in an attempt to complete any play;

Rule 5.09(a)(13) Comment: The objective of this rule is to penalize the offensive team for deliberate, unwarranted, unsportsmanlike action by the runner in leaving the baseline for the obvious purpose of crashing the pivot man on a double play, rather than trying to reach the base. Obviously this is an umpire's judgment play. (*See* Rule 6.01(j).)

(14) With two out, a runner on third base, and two strikes on the batter, the runner attempts to steal home base on a legal pitch and the ball touches the runner in the batter's strike zone. The umpire shall call "Strike Three," the batter is out and the run shall not count; before two are out, the umpire shall call "Strike Three," the ball is dead, and the run counts;

(15) A member of his team (other than a runner) hinders a fielder's attempt to catch or field a batted ball. *See* Rule 6.01(b). For interference by a runner, *see* Rule 5.09(b)(3).

(b) **Retiring a Runner**

Any runner is out when:

(1) He runs more than three feet away from his base path to avoid being tagged unless his action is to avoid interference with a fielder fielding a batted ball. A runner's base path is established when the tag attempt occurs and is a straight line from the runner to the base he is attempting to reach safely; or

(2) After touching first base, he leaves the base path, obviously abandoning his effort to touch the next base;

Rule 5.09(b)(1) and (2) Comment: Any runner after reaching first base who leaves the base path heading for his dugout or his position believing that there is no further play, may be declared out if the umpire judges the act of the runner to be considered abandoning his efforts to run the bases. Even though an out is called, the ball remains in play in regard to any other runner.

This rule also covers the following and similar plays: Less than two out, score tied last of ninth inning, runner on first, batter hits a ball out of park for winning run, the runner on first passes second and thinking the home run automatically wins the game, cuts across diamond toward his bench as batter-runner circles bases. In this case, the base runner would be called out "for abandoning his effort to touch the next base" and batter-runner permitted to continue around bases to make his home run valid. If there are two out, home run would not count. *See* Rule 5.09(d). This is not an appeal play.

> *PLAY*—Runner believing he is called out on a tag at first or third base starts for the dugout and progresses a reasonable distance still indicating by his actions that he is out, shall be declared out for abandoning the bases.

    (3) He intentionally interferes with a thrown ball; or hinders a fielder attempting to make a play on a batted ball (*see* Rule 6.01(j));

PENALTY: For penalties applying to a runner's intentional interference with a thrown ball or his hindrance of a fielder's attempt to make a play on a batted ball, *see* Rule 6.01(a) Penalty for Interference Comment.

    (4) He is tagged, when the ball is alive, while off his base.

EXCEPTION: A batter-runner cannot be tagged out after overrunning or oversliding first base if he returns immediately to the base;

APPROVED RULING: (A) If the impact of a runner breaks a base loose from its position, no play can be made on that runner at that base if he had reached the base safely.

APPROVED RULING: (B) If a base is dislodged from its position during a play, any following runner on the same play shall be considered as touching or occupying the base if, in the umpire's judgment, he touches or occupies the point marked by the dislodged bag.

(5) He fails to retouch his base after a fair or foul ball is legally caught before he, or his base, is tagged by a fielder. He shall not be called out for failure to retouch his base after the first following pitch, or any play or attempted play. This is an appeal play;

Rule 5.09(b)(5) Comment: Runners need not "tag up" on a foul tip. They may steal on a foul tip. If a so-called tip is not caught, it becomes an ordinary foul. Runners then return to their bases.

(6) He or the next base is tagged before he touches the next base, after he has been forced to advance by reason of the batter becoming a runner. However, if a following runner is put out on a force play, the force is removed and the runner must be tagged to be put out. The force is removed as soon as the runner touches the base to which he is forced to advance, and if he overslides or overruns the base, the runner must be tagged to be put out. However, if the forced runner, after touching the next base, retreats for any reason towards the base he had last occupied, the force play is reinstated, and he can again be put out if the defense tags the base to which he is forced;

Rule 5.09(b)(6) Comment:

PLAY—Runner on first and three balls on batter: Runner steals on the next pitch, which is fourth ball, but after having touched second he overslides or overruns that base. Catcher's throw catches him before he can return. Ruling is that runner is out. (Force out is removed.)

Oversliding and overrunning situations arise at bases other than first base. For instance, before two are out, and runners on first and second, or first, second and third, the ball is hit to an infielder who tries for the double play. The runner on first beats the throw to second base but over-slides the base. The relay is made to first base and the batter-runner is out. The first baseman, seeing the runner at second base off the bag, makes the return throw to second and the runner is tagged off the base. Meanwhile runners have crossed the plate. The question is: Is this a force play? Was the force removed when the batter-runner was out at first base? Do the runs that crossed the plate during this play and before the third out was made when the runner was tagged at second, count? Answer: The runs score. It is not a force play. It is a tag play.

(7) He is touched by a fair ball in fair territory before the ball has gone through, or by, an infielder and no other infielder has a chance to make a play on the ball. The ball is dead and no runner may score, nor runners advance, except runners forced to advance. EXCEPTION: If a runner is touching his base when touched by an Infield Fly, he is not out, although the batter is out;

Rule 5.09(b)(7) Comment: If two runners are touched by the same fair ball, only the first one is out because the ball is instantly dead.

If a runner is touched by an Infield Fly when he is not touching his base, and before the ball has gone through, or by, an infielder, and no other infielder has a chance to make a play on the ball, both the runner and batter are out. Regardless of whether a runner is touching his base or not when touched by an Infield Fly before the ball has gone through, or by, an infielder and no other infielder has a chance to make a play on the ball, the ball is dead and no runner may score, nor runners advance, except runners forced to advance.

(8) He attempts to score on a play in which the batter interferes with the play at home base before two are out. With two out, the interference puts the batter out and no score counts;

(9) He passes a preceding runner before such runner is out;

Rule 5.09(b)(9) Comment: A runner may be deemed to have passed a preceding (i.e., lead) runner based on his actions *or* the actions of a preceding runner.

PLAY—Runners on second base and third base with one out. The runner from third base (i.e., the lead runner) makes an advance toward home and is caught in a rundown between third base and home plate. Believing the lead runner will be tagged out, the runner at second base (i.e., the trailing runner) advances to third base. Before being tagged, the lead runner runs back to and beyond third base toward left field. At this time, the trailing runner has passed the lead runner as a result of the lead runner's actions. As a result, the trailing runner is out and third base is unoccupied. The lead runner is entitled to third base if he returns to touch it before he is out, *see* Rule 5.06(a)(1), unless he is declared out for abandoning the bases.

(10) After he has acquired legal possession of a base, he runs the bases in reverse order for the purpose of confusing the defense or making a travesty of the game. The umpire shall immediately call "Time" and declare the runner out;

Rule 5.09(b)(10) Comment: If a runner touches an unoccupied base and then thinks the ball was caught or is decoyed into returning to the base he last touched, he may be put out running back to that base, but if he reaches the previously occupied base safely he cannot be put out while in contact with that base.

(11) He fails to return at once to first base after overrunning or oversliding that base. If he attempts to run to second he is out when tagged. If, after overrunning or oversliding first base he starts toward the dugout, or toward his position, and fails to return to first base at once, he is out, on appeal, when he or the base is tagged;

Rule 5.09(b)(11) Comment: Runner who touches first base in overrunning and is declared safe by the umpire has, within the intent of Rule 5.08(a) "reached first base" and any run which scores on such a play counts, even though the runner subsequently becomes the third out for failure to return "at once," as covered in Rule 5.09(b)(11).

(12) In running or sliding for home base, he fails to touch home base and makes no attempt to return to the base,

when a fielder holds the ball in his hand, while touching home base, and appeals to the umpire for the decision;

Rule 5.09(b)(12) Comment: This rule applies only where runner is on his way to the bench and the catcher would be required to chase him. It does not apply to the ordinary play where the runner misses the plate and then immediately makes an effort to touch the plate before being tagged. In that case, runner must be tagged.

(13) A play on him is being made and a member of his team (other than a runner) hinders a fielder's attempt to field a thrown ball. *See* Rule 5.09(b)(3). For interference by a runner, *see* Rule 5.09(b)(3).

(c) **Appeal Plays**

Any runner shall be called out, on appeal, when:

(1) After a fly ball is caught, he fails to retouch his original base before he or his original base is tagged;

Rule 5.09(c)(1) Comment: "Retouch," in this rule, means to tag up and start from a contact with the base after the ball is caught. A runner is not permitted to take a flying start from a position in back of his base. Such runner shall be called out on appeal.

(2) With the ball in play, while advancing or returning to a base, he fails to touch each base in order before he, or a missed base, is tagged;

APPROVED RULING: (A) No runner may return to touch a missed base after a following runner has scored. (B) When the ball is dead, no runner may return to touch a missed base or one he has left after he has advanced to and touched a base beyond the missed base.

Rule 5.09(c)(2) Comment:

PLAY—(A) Batter hits ball out of park or ground rule double and misses first base (ball is dead)—he may return to first base to correct his mistake before he touches second but if he touches second he may not return to first and if defensive team appeals he is declared out at first.

PLAY—(B) Batter hits ball to shortstop who throws wild into stand (ball is dead)—batter-runner misses first base but is awarded second base on the overthrow. Even though the umpire has awarded the runner second base on the overthrow, the runner must touch first base before he proceeds to second base.

These are appeal plays.

(3) He overruns or overslides first base and fails to return to the base immediately, and he or the base is tagged prior to the runner returning to first base;

(4) He fails to touch home base and makes no attempt to return to that base, and home base is tagged.

Any appeal under this rule must be made before the next pitch, or any play or attempted play. If the violation occurs during a play which ends a half-inning, the appeal must be made before the defensive team leaves the field.

An appeal is not to be interpreted as a play or an attempted play.

Successive appeals may not be made on a runner at the same base. If the defensive team on its first appeal errs, a request for a second appeal on the same runner at the same base shall not be allowed by the umpire. (Intended meaning of the word "err" is that the defensive team in making an appeal threw the ball out of play. For example, if the pitcher threw to first base to appeal and threw the ball into the stands, no second appeal would be allowed.)

Appeal plays may require an umpire to recognize an apparent "fourth out." If the third out is made during a play in which an appeal play is sustained on another runner, the appeal play decision takes precedence in determining the out. If there is more than one appeal during a play that ends a half-inning, the defense may elect to take the out that gives it the advantage. For the purpose of this rule, the defensive team has "left the field" when the pitcher and all infielders have left fair territory on their way to the bench or Clubhouse.

Rule 5.09(c) Comment: If two runners arrive at home base about the same time and the first runner misses home plate but a second runner legally touches the plate, the runner is tagged out on his attempt to come back and touch the base or is called out, on appeal, then he shall be considered as having been put out before the second runner scored and being the third out. Second runner's run shall not count, as provided in Rule 5.09(d).

If a pitcher balks when making an appeal, such act shall be a play. An appeal should be clearly intended as an appeal, either by a verbal request by the player or an act that unmistakably indicates an appeal to the umpire. A player, inadvertently stepping on the base with a ball in his hand, would not constitute an appeal. Time is not out when an appeal is being made.

(d) **Effect of Preceding Runner's Failure to Touch a Base**

Unless two are out, the status of a following runner is not affected by a preceding runner's failure to touch or retouch a base. If, upon appeal, the preceding runner is the third out, no runners following him shall score. If such third out is the result of a force play, neither preceding nor following runners shall score.

(e) **Retiring the Side**

When three offensive players are legally put out, that team takes the field and the opposing team becomes the offensive team.

5.10 Substitutions and Pitching Changes (Including Visits to the Mound)

(a) A player, or players, may be substituted during a game at any time the ball is dead. A substitute player shall bat in the replaced player's position in the team's batting order.

(b) The manager shall immediately notify the umpire-in-chief of any substitution and shall state to the umpire-in-chief the substitute's place in the batting order.

Rule 5.10(b) Comment: To avoid any confusion, the manager should give the name of the substitute, his position in the batting order and his position on the field. When two or more substitute players of the defensive team enter the game at the same time, the manager shall, immediately before they take their positions as fielders, designate to the umpire-in-chief such players' positions in the team's batting order, and the umpire-in-chief shall so notify the Official Scorer. If this information is not immediately given to the umpire-in-chief, the umpire-in-chief shall have authority to designate the substitutes' places in the batting order.

If a double-switch is being made, the manager or coach shall first notify the plate umpire. The umpire-in-chief must be informed of the multiple substitutions and interchanged batting order before the manager calls for a new pitcher (regardless of whether the manager or coach announces the double-switch before crossing the foul line). Signaling or motioning to the bullpen is to be considered an official substitution for the new pitcher. It is not permissible for the manager to go to the mound, call for a new pitcher, and then inform the umpire of multiple substitutions with the intention of interchanging the batting order.

Players for whom substitutions have been made may remain with their team on the bench or may "warm-up" pitchers. If a manager substitutes another player for himself, he may continue to direct his team from the bench or the coach's box. Umpires should not permit players for whom substitutes have been made, and who are permitted to remain on the bench, to address any remarks to any opposing player or manager, or to the umpires.

(c) The umpire-in-chief, after having been notified, shall immediately announce, or cause to be announced, each substitution.

(d) A player once removed from a game shall not re-enter that game. If a player who has been substituted for attempts to re-enter, or re-enters, the game in any capacity, the umpire-in-chief shall direct the player's manager to remove such player from the game immediately upon noticing the player's presence or upon being informed of the player's improper presence by another umpire or by either manager. If such direction to remove the substituted for player occurs before play commences with the player improperly in the game, then the substitute player may enter the game. If such direction to remove the substituted-for player occurs after play has commenced with the substituted-for player in the game, then the substitute player shall be deemed to have been removed from the game (in addition to the removal of the substituted-for player) and shall not enter the game. If a substitute enters the game in place of a player-manager, the manager may thereafter go to the coaching lines at his discretion. When two or more substitute players of the defensive team enter the game at the same time, the manager shall, immediately before they take their positions as fielders, designate to the umpire-in-chief such players' positions in the team's batting order and the umpire-in-chief shall so notify the Official Scorer. If this information is not immediately given to the umpire-in-chief, he shall have authority to designate the substitutes' places in the batting order.

Rule 5.10(d) Comment: A pitcher may change to another position only once during the same inning; e.g. the pitcher will not be allowed to assume a position other than a pitcher more than once in the same inning.

Any player other than a pitcher substituted for an injured player shall be allowed five warm-up throws. (*See* Rule 5.07(b) for pitchers.)

Any play that occurs while a player appears in a game after having been substituted for shall count. If, in an umpire's judgment, the player re-entered the game knowing that he had been removed, the umpire may eject the manager.

(e) A player whose name is on his team's batting order may not become a substitute runner for another member of his team.

Rule 5.10(e) Comment: This rule is intended to eliminate the practice of using so-called courtesy runners. No player in the game shall be permitted to act as a courtesy runner for a teammate. No player who has been in the game and has been taken out for a substitute shall return as a courtesy runner. Any player not in the lineup, if used as a runner, shall be considered as a substitute player.

(f) The pitcher named in the batting order handed the umpire-in-chief, as provided in Rules 4.02(a) and 4.02(b), shall pitch to the first batter or any substitute batter until such batter is put out or reaches first base, unless the pitcher sustains injury or illness which, in the judgment of the umpire-in-chief, incapacitates him from pitching.

(g) **Minimum Batters Faced Requirements**

(1) The starting pitcher or any substitute pitcher is required to pitch to a minimum of three consecutive batters, including the batter then at bat (or any substitute batter), until such batters are put out or reach first base, or until the offensive team is put out, unless the starting pitcher or substitute pitcher sustains injury or illness which, in the umpire-in-chief's judgment, incapacitates him from further play as a pitcher.

Rule 5.10(g)(1) Comment: To qualify as one of three consecutive batters, the batter must complete his plate appearance, which ends only when the batter is put out or becomes a runner. If the offensive team is put out prior to any substitute pitcher completing his first three consecutive batters, the pitcher may be removed from the game between innings; but, if he returns for the subsequent inning, he must complete pitching to as many batters as necessary to satisfy the three consecutive batters requirement, which total would include any batters that completed a plate appearance with that pitcher the prior inning (i.e., if he completed 0 PA in inning 1, he must complete 3 PA in inning 2; if he completed 1 PA in inning 1, he must complete 2 PA in inning 2; if he completed 2 PA in inning 1, he must complete 1 PA in inning 2). An intentional walk counts toward fulfilling the number of required batters. Picking off a runner does not fulfill the minimum batter requirement, but would permit the early removal of the pitcher if the out recorded by the pickoff ends the inning.

(2) Any pitcher who warms up on the field at the start of an inning is required to pitch to at least the first batter of the inning until such batter (or any substitute batter) is put out or reaches first base, unless the pitcher sustains injury or illness which, in the umpire-in-chief's judgment, incapacitates him from further play as a pitcher.

Rule 5.10(g)(2) Comment: A league may provide standards to determine the pitcher that is subject to Rule 5.10(g)(2) in the event there is no pitcher warming up on the field at the start of an inning.

(h) If an improper substitution is made for the pitcher, the umpire shall direct the proper pitcher to return to the game until the provisions of this rule are fulfilled. If the improper pitcher is permitted to pitch, any play that results is legal. The improper pitcher becomes the proper pitcher as soon as he makes his first pitch to the batter, or as soon as any runner is put out.

Rule 5.10(h) Comment: If a manager attempts to remove a pitcher in violation of Rule 5.10(h) the umpire shall notify the manager of the offending Club that it cannot be done. If, by chance, the umpire-in-chief has, through oversight, announced the incoming improper pitcher, he should still correct the situation before the improper pitcher pitches. Once the improper pitcher delivers a pitch he becomes the proper pitcher.

(i) If a pitcher who is already in the game crosses the foul line on his way to take his place on the pitcher's plate to start an inning, he shall pitch to the first batter until such batter is put out or reaches first base, unless the batter is substituted for, or the pitcher sustains an injury or illness which, in the judgment of the umpire-in-chief, incapacitates him from pitching. If the pitcher ends the previous inning on base or at bat and does not return to the dugout after the inning is completed, the pitcher is not required to pitch to the first batter of the inning until he makes contact with the pitcher's plate to begin his warm-up pitches.

NOTE: The substitute batter exception to the requirement that a pitcher already in the game must face the first batter to start an inning contained in Rule 5.10(i) does not apply to a substitute pitcher who returns for a subsequent inning without having satisfied the three batter requirement contained in Rule 5.10(g). Thus, if a pitcher who has not completed his three batter requirement at the end of an inning returns for the subsequent inning, the obligation to satisfy the balance of this requirement shall continue even if the opposing team elects to pinch hit for the first hitter to start a subsequent inning.

(j) If no announcement of a substitution is made, the substitute shall be considered as having entered the game when:

(1) If a pitcher, he takes his place on the pitcher's plate;

(2) If a batter, he takes his place in the batter's box;

(3) If a fielder, he reaches the position usually occupied by the fielder he has replaced, and play commences;

(4) If a runner, he takes the place of the runner he has replaced.

Any play made by, or on, any of the above mentioned unannounced substitutes shall be legal.

(k) Players and substitutes of both teams shall confine themselves to their team's benches unless actually participating in the play or preparing to enter the game, or coaching at first or third base. Players, managers, coaches, trainers, and other Club personnel permitted to occupy the bench or bullpen area during the game may not enter the field of play unless actually participating in the play, preparing to enter the game, or another permissible reason (e.g., coaching at first or third base, mound visit).

PENALTY: For violation the umpire may, after warning, remove the offender from the field.

Rule 5.10(k) Comment: Players on the injured list are permitted to participate in pre-game activity and sit on the bench during a game but may not take part in any activity during the game such as warming up a pitcher, bench-jockeying, etc. Injured players are not allowed to enter the playing surface at any time or for any purpose during the game.

(l) Visits to the Mound Requiring a Pitcher's Removal From the Game

A professional league shall adopt the following rule pertaining to the visit of the manager or coach to the pitcher:

(1) This rule limits the number of trips a manager or coach may make to any one pitcher in any one inning;

(2) A second trip to the same pitcher in the same inning will cause this pitcher's automatic removal from the game;

(3) The manager or coach is prohibited from making a second visit to the mound while the same batter is at bat, but

(4) if a pinch-hitter is substituted for this batter, the manager or coach may make a second visit to the mound, but must remove the pitcher from the game.

A manager or coach is considered to have concluded his visit to the mound when he leaves the 18-foot circle surrounding the pitcher's rubber.

Rule 5.10(l) Comment: If the manager or coach goes to the catcher or infielder and that player then goes to the mound or the pitcher comes to him at his position before there is an intervening play (a pitch or other play) that will be the same as the manager or coach going to the mound.

Any attempt to evade or circumvent this rule by the manager or coach going to the catcher or an infielder and then that player going to the mound to confer with the pitcher shall constitute a trip to the mound.

If the coach goes to the mound and removes a pitcher and then the manager goes to the mound to talk with the new pitcher, that will constitute one trip to that new pitcher that inning.

A manager or coach shall not be considered to have concluded his visit to the mound if he temporarily leaves the 18-foot circle surrounding the pitcher's rubber for purposes of notifying the umpire that a double-switch or substitution is being made.

In a case where a manager has made his first trip to the mound and then returns the second time to the mound in the same inning with the same pitcher in the game and the same batter at bat, after being warned by the umpire that he cannot return to the mound, the manager shall be removed from the game and the pitcher required to pitch to the batter until he is retired or gets on base. After the batter is retired, or becomes a base runner, then this pitcher must be removed from the game. The manager should be notified that his pitcher will be removed from the game after he pitches to one hitter, so he can have a substitute pitcher warmed up. In such circumstance, the substitute pitcher will be allowed as much time to throw preparatory pitches as in the umpire's judgment circumstances justify.

For purposes of this Rule 5.10(*l*), replacing the pitcher shall constitute one trip to that pitcher that inning, regardless of whether the manager or coach chooses to go to the mound, or whether the pitcher remains in the game at a different position on defense.

(m) Limitation on the Number of Mound Visits Per Game

The following rule shall apply in Major League games. The Minor Leagues may adopt a rule providing for a different limitation on the number of mound visits permitted in a game or no limitation on the number of mound visits.

(1) Mound visits without a pitching change shall be limited to four per team, per nine innings. For any extra inning played, each team shall be entitled to one additional non-pitching-change mound visit in that inning, which if not used in that inning, will not carry over to any subsequent extra inning played.

(2) For purposes of this Rule 5.10(m), a manager or coach trip to the mound to meet with the pitcher shall constitute a visit. A player leaving his position to confer with the pitcher, including a pitcher leaving the mound to confer with another player, shall also constitute a visit, regardless of where the visit occurs or the length of the visit. Visits by a manager, coach or player to join a mound visit already in progress shall not constitute an independent visit. In addition, the following shall not constitute visits:

(A) Discussions between pitchers and position player(s) that occur between batters in the normal course of play and do not require either the position player(s) or the pitcher to relocate;

(B) Visits by position players to the mound solely to clean spikes, provided the player does not confer with the pitcher;

(C) Visits to the mound due to an injury or potential injury of the pitcher;

(D) Visits by position players to the mound after the announcement of an offensive substitution but prior to a subsequent pitch or play;

(E) Visits to the mound by position players that occur during a suspension of play pursuant to an umpire's call of "Time" (e.g., following an injury to an umpire or player; the presence of a spectator, object, or a member of the grounds crew on the field; a manager's initiation of Replay Review, etc.), provided that the mound visit does not otherwise delay a return to game action;

(F) Visits to the mound by position players after a home run, provided that the player returns to his position before the runner crosses home plate; and

(G) Visits to the mound by position players during an inning break or pitching change, provided that the mound visit does not prevent the pitcher from complying with any applicable inning break or pitching change time limits.

(3) Cross Up in Signs. In the event a team has exhausted its allotment of mound visits in a game (or extra inning) and the home plate umpire determines that the catcher and pitcher did not have a shared understanding of the location or type of pitch that had been signaled by the catcher (otherwise referred to as a "cross up"), the home plate umpire may, upon request of the catcher, allow the catcher to make a brief mound visit. However, any mound visit resulting from a "cross up" prior to a team exhausting its allotted number of visits shall count against a team's total number of allotted mound visits.

(4) Enforcement of Mound Visit Limits. A manager or coach who crosses the foul line on his way to the mound after his team has exhausted its mound visits must make a pitching change, unless the pitcher has not pitched to a minimum of three consecutive batters in accordance with Rule 5.10(g),

in which case the pitcher shall continue to pitch only to complete pitching to his first three consecutive batters (or the end of the inning, whichever comes first) in accordance with Rule 5.10(g). If a manager or coach believes an exception to the mound visit rule applies, he must confer with the umpire prior to crossing the foul line. In circumstances in which a team is forced to make an unintended pitching change by operation of this Rule, and there is no relief pitcher warming up in the bullpen, the manager or coach who violated the Rule by exceeding his team's allotted number of mound visits shall be subject to ejection from the game. The umpire may allow the substitute pitcher additional time to prepare to enter the game.

If a position player makes a visit after his team has exhausted its allotted number of mound visits he may be subject to ejection for failing to return to his position when instructed by the umpire; however, an impermissible visit by a position player shall not require the removal of the pitcher.

5.11 Designated Hitter Rule

(a) The Designated Hitter Rule provides as follows:

(1) A hitter may be designated to bat for the starting pitcher and all subsequent pitchers in any game without otherwise affecting the status of the pitcher(s) in the game. A Designated Hitter for the pitcher, if any, must be selected prior to the game and must be included in the lineup cards presented to the umpire-in-chief. If a manager lists 10 players in his team's lineup card, but fails to indicate one as the Designated Hitter, and an umpire or either manager (or designee of either manager who presents his team's lineup card) notices the error before the umpire-in-chief calls "Play" to start the game, the umpire-in-chief shall direct the manager who had made the omission to designate which of the nine players, other than the pitcher, will be the Designated Hitter.

Rule 5.11(a)(1) Comment: A correction of a failure to indicate a Designated Hitter when 10 players are listed in a batting order is an "obvious" error that may be corrected before a game starts. *See* Rule 4.03 Comment.

(2) The Designated Hitter named in the starting lineup must come to bat at least one time, unless the opposing Club changes pitchers.

(3) It is not mandatory that a Club designate a hitter for the pitcher, but failure to do so prior to the game precludes the use of a Designated Hitter for that Club for that game.

(4) Pinch-hitters for a Designated Hitter may be used. Any substitute hitter for a Designated Hitter becomes the Designated Hitter. A replaced Designated Hitter shall not re-enter the game in any capacity.

(5) The Designated Hitter may be used on defense, continuing to bat in the same position in the batting order, but the pitcher must then bat in the place of the substituted defensive player, unless more than one substitution is made, and the manager then must designate their spots in the batting order.

(6) A runner may be substituted for the Designated Hitter and the runner assumes the role of Designated Hitter. A Designated Hitter may not pinch-run.

(7) A Designated Hitter is "locked" into the batting order. No multiple substitutions may be made that will alter the batting rotation of the Designated Hitter.

(8) Once the game pitcher is switched from the mound to a position on defense, such move shall terminate the Designated Hitter role for that Club for the remainder of the game.

(9) Once a pinch-hitter bats for any player in the batting order and then enters the game to pitch, such move shall terminate the Designated Hitter role for that Club for the remainder of the game.

(10) Once the game pitcher bats or runs for the Designated Hitter, such move shall terminate the Designated Hitter

role for that Club for the remainder of the game. The game pitcher may pinch-hit or pinch-run only for the Designated Hitter.

(11) If a manager lists 10 players in his team's lineup card, but fails to indicate one as the Designated Hitter, and the opposing manager brings the failure to list a Designated Hitter to the attention of the umpire-in-chief after the game starts, then

(A) the pitcher will be required to bat in the batting order in the place of the listed player who has not assumed a position on defense, if the team has taken the field on defense, or

(B) if the team has not yet taken the field on defense, the pitcher will be placed in the batting order in place of any player, as chosen by the manager of that team.

In either case, the player whom the pitcher replaces in the batting order shall be considered to have been substituted for and is removed from the game and the Designated Hitter role for that Club shall be terminated for the remainder of the game. Any play that occurred before the violation is brought to the attention of the umpire-in-chief shall count, subject to Rule 6.03(b).

(12) Once a Designated Hitter assumes a position on defense, such move shall terminate the Designated Hitter role for that Club for the remainder of the game.

(13) A substitute for the Designated Hitter need not be announced until it is the Designated Hitter's turn to bat.

(14) If a player on defense goes to the mound (i.e., replaces the pitcher), this move shall terminate the Designated Hitter's role for that Club for the remainder of the game.

(15) The Designated Hitter may not sit in the bullpen unless serving as a catcher in the bullpen.

(b) **Starting Pitcher as Designated Hitter.** It is not mandatory that a Club designate a hitter for the pitcher. However, in the event the starting pitcher will bat for himself, the player will be considered

63

two separate people for purposes of Rule 5.11(a). In such cases, the manager should list 10 players on his team's lineup card, and this player should be named twice – once as the starting pitcher and once as the Designated Hitter. Thus, if the starting pitcher is replaced, he can continue as the Designated Hitter (but can no longer pitch in the game), and if the Designated Hitter is replaced, he can continue as the pitcher (but can no longer hit for himself). If the player is simultaneously replaced both as a starting pitcher and Designated Hitter, he cannot be replaced by another two-way player filling both roles as separate people (this can be done only once on the initial lineup card by identifying that the starting pitcher will bat for himself).

Notwithstanding anything to the contrary in Rule 5.11(a) above, if that pitcher bats or runs as Designated Hitter, such move will not terminate the Designated Hitter role for that Club; neither will the role be terminated in the event that Designated Hitter assumes the role of pitcher on defense. However, if that player is switched from the mound or Designated Hitter role to a position on defense other than pitcher, such move will terminate the Designated Hitter role for that Club for the remainder of the game.

5.12 Calling "Time" and Dead Balls

(a) When an umpire suspends play, he shall call "Time." At the umpire-in-chief's call of "Play," the suspension is lifted and play resumes. Between the call of "Time" and the call of "Play" the ball is dead.

(b) The ball becomes dead when an umpire calls "Time." The umpire-in-chief shall call "Time:

  (1) When in his judgment weather, darkness or similar conditions make immediate further play impossible;

  (2) When light failure makes it difficult or impossible for the umpires to follow the play;

  NOTE: A league may adopt its own regulations governing games interrupted by light failure.

  (3) When an accident incapacitates a player or an umpire;

(A) If an accident to a runner is such as to prevent him from proceeding to a base to which he is entitled, as on a home run hit out of the playing field, or an award of one or more bases, a substitute runner shall be permitted to complete the play.

(4) When a manager requests "Time" for a substitution, or for a conference with one of his players.

(5) When the umpire wishes to examine the ball, to consult with either manager, or for any similar cause.

(6) When a fielder, after catching a fly ball, steps or falls into any out-of-play area. All other runners shall advance one base, without liability to be put out, from his last legally touched base at the time the fielder entered such out-of-play area.

(7) When an umpire orders a player or any other person removed from the playing field.

(8) Except in the cases stated in paragraphs (2) and (3)(A) of this rule, no umpire shall call "Time" while a play is in progress.

After the ball is dead, play shall be resumed when the pitcher takes his place on the pitcher's plate with a new ball or the same ball in his possession and the plate umpire calls "Play." The plate umpire shall call "Play" as soon as the pitcher takes his place on his plate with the ball in his possession.

6.00–IMPROPER PLAY, ILLEGAL ACTION, AND MISCONDUCT

6.01 Interference, Obstruction, and Catcher Collisions

(a) Batter or Runner Interference

It is interference by a batter or a runner when:

(1) After a third strike that is not caught by the catcher, the batter-runner clearly hinders the catcher in his attempt to field the ball. Such batter-runner is out, the ball is dead, and all other runners return to the bases they occupied at the time of the pitch. If a pitch that is not caught remains in the vicinity of home plate and it is inadvertently deflected by the batter or umpire, that ball is a dead ball and the runners should return to the bases they occupied at the time of the pitch (but if the pitch was strike three, the batter is out).

Rule 6.01(a)(1) Comment: If the pitched ball deflects off the catcher or umpire and subsequently touches the batter-runner, it is not considered interference unless, in the judgment of the umpire, the batter-runner clearly hinders the catcher in his attempt to field the ball.

(2) He intentionally deflects the course of a foul ball in any manner;

(3) Before two are out and a runner on third base, the batter hinders a fielder in making a play at home base; the runner is out;

(4) Any member or members of the offensive team stand or gather around any base to which a runner is advancing, to confuse, hinder or add to the difficulty of the fielders. Such runner shall be declared out for the interference of his teammate or teammates;

(5) Any batter or runner who has just been put out, or any runner who has just scored, hinders or impedes any following play being made on a runner. Such runner shall be declared out for the interference of his teammate (*see* Rule 6.01(j));

Rule 6.01(a)(5) Comment: If the batter or a runner continues to advance or returns or attempts to return to his last legally touched base after he has been put out, he shall not by that act alone be considered as confusing, hindering or impeding the fielders.

(6) If, in the judgment of the umpire, a base runner willfully and deliberately interferes with a batted ball or a fielder in the act of fielding a batted ball with the obvious intent to break up a double play, the ball is dead. The umpire shall call the runner out for interference and also call out the batter-runner because of the action of his teammate. In no event may bases be run or runs scored because of such action by a runner (*see* Rule 6.01(j));

(7) If, in the judgment of the umpire, a batter-runner willfully and deliberately interferes with a batted ball or a fielder in the act of fielding a batted ball, with the obvious intent to break up a double play, the ball is dead; the umpire shall call the batter-runner out for interference and shall call out the runner who had advanced closest to the home plate regardless where the double play might have been possible. In no event shall bases be run because of such interference (*see* Rule 6.01(j));

(8) In the judgment of the umpire, the base coach at third base, or first base, by touching or holding the runner, physically assists him in returning to or leaving third base or first base;

(9) With a runner on third base, the base coach leaves his box and acts in any manner to draw a throw by a fielder;

(10) He fails to avoid a fielder who is attempting to field a batted ball, or intentionally interferes with a thrown ball, provided that if two or more fielders attempt to field a batted ball, and the runner comes in contact with one or more of them, the umpire shall determine which fielder is entitled to the benefit of this rule, and shall not declare the runner out for coming in contact with a fielder other than the one the umpire determines to be entitled to field such a ball. The umpire shall call the runner out in accordance with Rule 5.09(b)(3). If the third out occurs because a

runner is declared out for interference on a foul batted ball, the batter-runner is considered to have completed his at bat, and the first batter up the following inning will be the player who follows him in the batting order (if there are less than two outs, the batter will complete his at-bat). If the batter-runner is adjudged not to have hindered a fielder attempting to make a play on a batted ball, and if the base runner's interference is adjudged not to be intentional, the batter-runner shall be awarded first base;

Rule 6.01(a)(10) Comment: When a catcher and batter-runner going to first base have contact when the catcher is fielding the ball, there is generally no violation and nothing should be called. "Obstruction" by a fielder attempting to field a ball should be called only in very flagrant and violent cases because the rules give him the right of way, but of course such "right of way" is not a license to, for example, intentionally trip a runner even though fielding the ball. If the catcher is fielding the ball and any fielder, including the pitcher, obstructs a runner going to first base, "obstruction" shall be called and the base runner awarded first base.

(11) A fair ball touches him on fair territory before touching a fielder. If a fair ball goes through, or by, an infielder, and touches a runner immediately back of him, or touches the runner after having been deflected by a fielder, the umpire shall not declare the runner out for being touched by a batted ball. In making such decision the umpire must be convinced that the ball passed through, or by, the fielder, and that no other infielder had the chance to make a play on the ball. If, in the judgment of the umpire, the runner deliberately and intentionally kicks such a batted ball on which the infielder has missed a play, then the runner shall be called out for interference.

PENALTY FOR INTERFERENCE:
The runner is out and the ball is dead.

If the umpire declares the batter, batter-runner, or a runner out for interference, all other runners shall return to the last base that was in the judgment of the umpire, legally touched at the time of the interference, unless otherwise provided by these rules.

In the event the batter-runner has not reached first base, all runners shall return to the base last occupied at the time of the pitch; provided, however, if during an intervening play at the plate with less than two outs a runner scores, and then the batter-runner is called out for interference outside (to the right of) the three-foot line, or inside (to the left of) the foul line and on the infield grass, in running the last half of the distance from home base to first base, the runner is safe and the run shall count.

Rule 6.01(a) Penalty for Interference Comment: A runner who is adjudged to have hindered a fielder who is attempting to make a play on a batted ball is out whether it was intentional or not.

If, however, the runner has contact with a legally occupied base when he hinders the fielder, he shall not be called out unless, in the umpire's judgment, such hindrance, whether it occurs on fair or foul territory, is intentional. If the umpire declares the hindrance intentional, the following penalty shall apply: With less than two out, the umpire shall declare both the runner and batter out. With two out, the umpire shall declare the batter out.

If, in a run-down between third base and home plate, the succeeding runner has advanced and is standing on third base when the runner in a run-down is called out for offensive interference, the umpire shall send the runner standing on third base back to second base.

This same principle applies if there is a run-down between second and third base and succeeding runner has reached second (the reasoning is that no runner shall advance on an interference play and a runner is considered to occupy a base until he legally has reached the next succeeding base).

(b) **Fielder Right of Way**

The players, coaches or any member of a team at bat shall vacate any space (including both dugouts or bullpens) needed by a fielder who is attempting to field a batted or thrown ball. If a member of the team at bat (other than a runner) hinders a fielder's attempt to catch or field a batted ball, the ball is dead, the batter is declared out and all runners return to the bases occupied at the time of the pitch. If a member of the team at bat (other than a runner) hinders a fielder's attempt to field a thrown ball, the ball is dead, the runner on whom the play is being made shall be declared out and all runners return to the last legally occupied base at the time of the interference.

Rule 6.01(b) Comment: Defensive interference is an act by a fielder that hinders or prevents a batter from hitting a pitch.

(c) Catcher Interference

The batter becomes a runner and is entitled to first base without liability to be put out (provided he advances to and touches first base) when the catcher or any fielder interferes with him. If a play follows the interference, the manager of the offense may advise the plate umpire that he elects to decline the interference penalty and accept the play. Such election shall be made immediately at the end of the play. However, if the batter reaches first base on a hit, an error, a base on balls, a hit batsman, or otherwise, and all other runners advance at least one base, the play proceeds without reference to the interference.

Rule 6.01(c) Comment: If catcher's interference is called with a play in progress the umpire will allow the play to continue because the manager may elect to take the play. If the batter-runner missed first base, or a runner misses his next base, he shall be considered as having reached the base, as stated in Note of Rule 5.06(b)(3)(D).

Examples of plays the manager might elect to take:

1. Runner on third, one out, batter hits fly ball to the outfield on which the runner scores but catcher's interference was called. The offensive manager may elect to take the run and have batter called out or have runner remain at third and batter awarded first base.

2. Runner on second base. Catcher interferes with batter. As he bunts ball fairly sending runner to third base. The

manager may rather have runner on third base with an out on the play than have runners on second and first.

If a runner is trying to score by a steal or squeeze from third base, note the additional penalty set forth in Rule 6.01(g).

If the catcher interferes with the batter before the pitcher delivers the ball, it shall not be considered interference on the batter under Rule 5.05(b)(3). In such cases, the umpire shall call "Time" and the pitcher and batter start over from "scratch."

(d) **Unintentional Interference**

In case of unintentional interference with play by any person herein authorized to be on the playing field (except members of the team at bat who are participating in the game, or a base coach, any of whom interfere with a fielder attempting to field a batted or thrown ball; or an umpire) the ball is alive and in play. If the interference is intentional, the ball shall be dead at the moment of the interference and the umpire shall impose such penalties as in his opinion will nullify the act of interference.

Rule 6.01(d) Comment: For interference with a fielder attempting to field a batted or thrown ball by members of the team at bat or base coaches, who are excepted in Rule 6.01(d), *see* Rule 6.01(b). *See also* Rules 5.06(c)(2), 5.06(c)(6) and 5.05(b)(4), which cover interference by an umpire, and Rule 5.09(b)(3), which covers interference by a runner.

The question of intentional or unintentional interference shall be decided on the basis of the person's action. For example: a bat boy, ball attendant, policeman, etc., who tries to avoid being touched by a thrown or batted ball but still is touched by the ball would be involved in unintentional interference. If, however, he picks up the ball, catches it, or touches the ball by intentionally pushing or kicking at the ball, this act would constitute intentional interference.

PLAY: Batter hits ball to shortstop, who fields ball but throws wild past the first baseman. The coach at first base, to avoid being hit by the ball, falls to the ground and the first baseman on his way to retrieve the wild thrown ball, runs into the coach. The batter-runner finally ends up on third base. Whether the umpire should call interference on the part of the coach is up to the judgment of the umpire and if the umpire felt that the coach did all he could to avoid interfering with the play, no interference need be called. If, in the judgment of the umpire, the coach was attempting to make it appear that he was trying not to interfere, the umpire should rule interference.

(e) Spectator Interference

When there is spectator interference with any thrown or batted ball, the ball shall be dead at the moment of interference and the umpire shall impose such penalties as in his opinion will nullify the act of interference.

> *APPROVED RULING:* If spectator interference clearly prevents a fielder from catching a fly ball, the umpire shall declare the batter out.

Rule 6.01(e) Comment: There is a difference between a ball which has been thrown or batted into the stands, touching a spectator thereby being out of play even though it rebounds onto the field and a spectator going onto the field or reaching over, under or through a barrier and touching a ball in play or touching or otherwise interfering with a player. In the latter case it is clearly intentional and shall be dealt with as intentional interference as in Rule 6.01(d). Batter and runners shall be placed where in the umpire's judgment they would have been had the interference not occurred.

No interference shall be allowed when a fielder reaches over a fence, railing, rope or into a stand to catch a ball. He does so at his own risk. However, should a spectator reach out on the playing field side of such fence, railing or rope, and plainly prevent the fielder from catching the ball, then the batsman should be called out for the spectator's interference.

EXAMPLE: Runner on third base, one out and a batter hits a fly ball deep to the outfield (fair or foul). Spectator clearly interferes with the outfielder attempting to catch the fly ball. Umpire calls the batter out for spectator interference. Ball is dead at the time of the call. Umpire decides that because of the distance the ball was hit, the runner on third base would have scored after the catch if the fielder had caught the ball which was interfered with, therefore, the runner is permitted to score. This might not be the case if such fly ball was interfered with a short distance from home plate.

(f) Coach and Umpire Interference

If a thrown ball accidentally touches a base coach, or a pitched or thrown ball touches an umpire, the ball is alive and in play. However, if the coach interferes with a thrown ball, the runner is out.

Rule 6.01(f) Comment: Umpire's interference occurs (1) when a plate umpire hinders, impedes or prevents a catcher's throw attempting to prevent a stolen base or retire a runner on a pick-off play; or (2) when a fair ball touches an umpire on fair territory before passing a fielder. Umpire interference may also occur when an umpire interferes with a catcher returning the ball to the pitcher.

(g) Interference With Squeeze Play or Steal of Home

If, with a runner on third base and trying to score by means of a squeeze play or a steal, the catcher or any other fielder steps on, or in front of home base without possession of the ball, or touches the batter or his bat, the pitcher shall be charged with a balk, the batter shall be awarded first base on the interference and the ball is dead.

(h) Obstruction

When obstruction occurs, the umpire shall call or signal "Obstruction."

(1) If a play is being made on the obstructed runner, or if the batter-runner is obstructed before he touches first base, the ball is dead and all runners shall advance, without liability to be put out, to the bases they would have reached, in the umpire's judgment, if there had been no obstruction. The obstructed runner shall be awarded at least one base beyond the base he had last legally touched before the

73

obstruction. Any preceding runners, forced to advance by the award of bases as the penalty for obstruction, shall advance without liability to be put out.

Rule 6.01(h)(1) Comment: When a play is being made on an obstructed runner, the umpire shall signal obstruction in the same manner that he calls "Time," with both hands overhead. The ball is immediately dead when this signal is given; however, should a thrown ball be in flight before the obstruction is called by the umpire, the runners are to be awarded such bases on wild throws as they would have been awarded had not obstruction occurred. On a play where a runner was trapped between second and third and obstructed by the third baseman going into third base while the throw is in flight from the shortstop, if such throw goes into the dugout the obstructed runner is to be awarded home base. Any other runners on base in this situation would also be awarded two bases from the base they last legally touched before obstruction was called.

(2) If no play is being made on the obstructed runner, the play shall proceed until no further action is possible. The umpire shall then call "Time" and impose such penalties, if any, as in his judgment will nullify the act of obstruction.

Rule 6.01(h)(2) Comment: Under Rule 6.01(h)(2), when the ball is not dead on obstruction and an obstructed runner advances beyond the base which, in the umpire's judgment, he would have been awarded because of being obstructed, he does so at his own peril and may be tagged out. This is a judgment call.

NOTE: The catcher, without the ball in his possession, has no right to block the pathway of the runner attempting to score. The base line belongs to the runner and the catcher should be there only when he is fielding a ball or when he already has the ball in his hand.

Rule 6.01(h) Comment: If a fielder is about to receive a thrown ball and if the ball is in flight directly toward and near enough to the fielder so he must occupy his position to receive the ball he may be considered "in the act of fielding a ball." It is entirely up to the judgment of the umpire as to whether a fielder is in the act of fielding a ball. After a fielder has made an attempt to field a ball and missed, he can no longer be in the "act of fielding" the ball. For example: An infielder dives at a ground ball and the ball passes him and he continues to lie on the ground and delays the progress of the runner, he very likely has obstructed the runner.

(i) **Collisions at Home Plate**

(1) A runner attempting to score may not deviate from his direct pathway to the plate in order to initiate contact with the catcher, or otherwise initiate an avoidable collision. If, in the judgment of the umpire, a runner attempting to score initiates contact with the catcher in such a manner, the umpire shall declare the runner out (regardless of whether the catcher maintains possession of the ball). In such circumstances, the umpire shall call the ball dead, and all other base runners shall return to the last base touched at the time of the collision. If the runner slides into the plate in an appropriate manner, he shall not be adjudged to have violated Rule 6.01(i).

Rule 6.01(i)(1) Comment: The failure by the runner to make an effort to touch the plate, the runner's lowering of the shoulder, or the runner's pushing through with his hands, elbows or arms, would support a determination that the runner deviated from the pathway in order to initiate contact with the catcher in violation of Rule 6.01(i), or otherwise initiated a collision that could have been avoided. A slide shall be deemed appropriate, in the case of a feet first slide, if the runner's buttocks and legs should hit the ground before contact with the catcher. In the case of a head first slide, a runner shall be deemed to have slid appropriately if his body should hit the ground before contact with the catcher. If a catcher blocks the pathway of the runner, the umpire shall not find that the runner initiated an avoidable collision in violation of this Rule 6.01(i)(1).

(2) Unless the catcher is in possession of the ball, the catcher cannot block the pathway of the runner as he is attempting to score. If, in the judgment of the umpire, the catcher

without possession of the ball blocks the pathway of the runner, the umpire shall call or signal the runner safe. Notwithstanding the above, it shall not be considered a violation of this Rule 6.01(i)(2) if the catcher blocks the pathway of the runner in a legitimate attempt to field the throw (e.g., in reaction to the direction, trajectory or the hop of the incoming throw, or in reaction to a throw that originates from a pitcher or drawn-in infielder). In addition, a catcher without possession of the ball shall not be adjudged to violate this Rule 6.01(i)(2) if the runner could have avoided the collision with the catcher (or other player covering home plate) by sliding.

Rule 6.01(i)(2) Comment: A catcher shall not be deemed to have violated Rule 6.01(i)(2) unless he has both blocked the plate without possession of the ball (or when not in a legitimate attempt to field the throw), and also hindered or impeded the progress of the runner attempting to score. A catcher shall not be deemed to have hindered or impeded the progress of the runner if, in the judgment of the umpire, the runner would have been called out notwithstanding the catcher having blocked the plate. In addition, a catcher should use best efforts to avoid unnecessary and forcible contact while tagging a runner attempting to slide. Catchers who routinely make unnecessary and forcible contact with a runner attempting to slide (e.g., by initiating contact using a knee, shin guard, elbow or forearm) may be subject to discipline by the Office of the Commissioner.

All references to "the catcher" in this Rule 6.01(i) shall apply equally to other players covering home plate. In addition, Rule 6.01(i)(2) shall not apply to force plays at home plate.

(j) Sliding to Bases on Double Play Attempts

If a runner does not engage in a bona fide slide, and initiates (or attempts to make) contact with the fielder for the purpose of breaking up a double play, he should be called for interference under this Rule 6.01. A "bona fide slide" for purposes of Rule 6.01 occurs when the runner:

(1) begins his slide (i.e., makes contact with the ground) before reaching the base;

(2) is able and attempts to reach the base with his hand or foot;

(3) is able and attempts to remain on the base (except home plate) after completion of the slide; and

(4) slides within reach of the base without changing his pathway for the purpose of initiating contact with a fielder.

A runner who engages in a "bona fide slide" shall not be called for interference under this Rule 6.01, even in cases where the runner makes contact with the fielder as a consequence of a permissible slide. In addition, interference shall not be called where a runner's contact with the fielder was caused by the fielder being positioned in (or moving into) the runner's legal pathway to the base.

Notwithstanding the above, a slide shall not be a "bona fide slide" if a runner engages in a "roll block," or intentionally initiates (or attempts to initiate) contact with the fielder by elevating and kicking his leg above the fielder's knee or throwing his arm or his upper body.

If the umpire determines that the runner violated this Rule 6.01(j), the umpire shall declare both the runner and batter-runner out. Note, however, that if the runner has already been put out then the runner on whom the defense was attempting to make a play shall be declared out.

6.02 Pitcher Illegal Action

(a) Balks

If there is a runner, or runners, it is a balk when:

(1) The pitcher, while touching his plate, makes any motion naturally associated with his pitch and fails to make such delivery;

Rule 6.02(a)(1) Comment: If a left-handed or right-handed pitcher swings his free foot past the back edge of the pitcher's rubber, he is required to pitch to the batter except to throw to second base on a pick-off play.

(2) The pitcher, while touching his plate, feints a throw to first or third base and fails to complete the throw;

(3) The pitcher, while touching his plate, fails to step directly toward a base before throwing to that base;

Rule 6.02(a)(3) Comment: Requires the pitcher, while touching his plate, to step directly toward a base before throwing to that base. If a pitcher turns or spins off of his free foot without actually stepping or if he turns his body and throws before stepping, it is a balk.

A pitcher is to step directly toward a base before throwing to that base and is required to throw (except to second base) because he steps. It is a balk if, with runners on first and third, the pitcher steps toward third and does not throw, merely to bluff the runner back to third; then seeing the runner on first start for second, turn and step toward and throw to first base. It is legal for a pitcher to feint a throw to second base.

(4) The pitcher, while touching his plate, throws, or feints a throw to an unoccupied base, except for the purpose of making a play;

Rule 6.02(a)(4) Comment: When determining whether the pitcher throws or feints a throw to an unoccupied base for the purpose of making a play, the umpire should consider whether a runner on the previous base demonstrates or otherwise creates an impression of his intent to advance to such unoccupied base.

(5) The pitcher makes an illegal pitch;

Rule 6.02(a)(5) Comment: A quick pitch is an illegal pitch. Umpires will judge a quick pitch as one delivered before the batter is reasonably set in the batter's box. With runners on base the penalty is a balk; with no runners on base, it is a ball. The quick pitch is dangerous and should not be permitted.

(6) The pitcher delivers the ball to the batter while he is not facing the batter;

(7) The pitcher makes any motion naturally associated with his pitch while he is not touching the pitcher's plate;

(8) The pitcher unnecessarily delays the game;

Rule 6.02(a)(8) Comment: Rule 6.02(a)(8) shall not apply when a warning is given pursuant to Rule 6.02(c)(8) (which prohibits intentional delay of a game by throwing to fielders not in an attempt to put a runner out). If a pitcher is ejected pursuant to Rule 6.02(c)(8) for continuing to delay the game, the penalty in Rule 6.02(a)(8) shall also apply. Rule 5.07(c) (which sets a time limit for a pitcher to deliver the ball when the bases are unoccupied) applies only when there are no runners on base.

(9) The pitcher, without having the ball, stands on or astride the pitcher's plate or while off the plate, he feints a pitch;

(10) The pitcher, after coming to a legal pitching position, removes one hand from the ball other than in an actual pitch, or in throwing to a base;

(11) The pitcher, while touching his plate, accidentally or intentionally has the ball slip or fall out of his hand or glove;

(12) The pitcher, while giving an intentional base on balls, pitches when the catcher is not in the catcher's box;

(13) The pitcher delivers the pitch from Set Position without coming to a stop.

PENALTY: The ball is dead, and each runner shall advance one base without liability to be put out, unless the batter reaches first on a hit, an error, a base on balls, a hit batter, or otherwise, and all other runners advance at least one base, in which case the play proceeds without reference to the balk.

APPROVED RULING: In cases where a pitcher balks and throws wild, either to a base or to home plate, a runner or runners may advance beyond the base to which he is entitled at his own risk.

APPROVED RULING: A runner who misses the first base to which he is advancing and who is called out on appeal shall be considered as having advanced one base for the purpose of this rule.

Rule 6.02(a) Comment: Umpires should bear in mind that the purpose of the balk rule is to prevent the pitcher from deliberately deceiving the base runner. If there is doubt in the umpire's mind, the "intent" of the pitcher should govern. However, certain specifics should be borne in mind:

(A) Straddling the pitcher's rubber without the ball is to be interpreted as intent to deceive and ruled a balk.

(B) With a runner on first base the pitcher may make a complete turn, without hesitating toward first, and throw to second. This is not to be interpreted as throwing to an unoccupied base.

(b) Illegal Pitches With Bases Unoccupied

If the pitcher makes an illegal pitch with the bases unoccupied, it shall be called a ball unless the batter reaches first base on a hit, an error, a base on balls, a hit batter or otherwise.

Rule 6.02(b) Comment: A ball which slips out of a pitcher's hand and crosses the foul line shall be called a ball; otherwise it will be called no pitch. This would be a balk with men on base.

(c) Pitching Prohibitions

The pitcher shall not:

(1) While in the 18-foot circle surrounding the pitcher's plate, touch the ball after touching his mouth or lips, or touch his mouth or lips while he is in contact with the pitcher's plate. The pitcher must clearly wipe the fingers of his pitching hand dry before touching the ball or the pitcher's plate.

EXCEPTION: Provided it is agreed to by both managers, the umpire prior to the start of a game played in cold weather, may permit the pitcher to blow on his hand.

PENALTY: For violation of this part of this rule the umpires shall immediately remove the ball from play and issue a warning to the pitcher. Any subsequent violation shall be called a ball. However, if the pitch is made and a batter reaches first base on a hit, an error, a hit batsman or otherwise, and no other runner is put out before advancing at least one base, the play shall proceed without reference to the violation. Repeat offenders shall be subject to a fine by the Office of the Commissioner.

(2) expectorate on the ball, either hand or his glove;

(3) rub the ball on his glove, person or clothing;

(4) apply a foreign substance of any kind to the ball;

(5) deface the ball in any manner; or

(6) deliver a ball altered in a manner prescribed by Rule 6.02(c) (2) through (5) or what is called the "shine" ball, "spit" ball, "mud" ball or "emery" ball. The pitcher is allowed to rub the ball between his bare hands.

(7) Have on his person, or in his possession, any foreign substance.

Rule 6.02(c)(7) Comment: The pitcher may not attach anything to either hand, any finger or either wrist (e.g., Band-Aid, tape, Super Glue, bracelet, etc.). The umpire shall determine if such attachment is indeed a foreign substance for the purpose of Rule 6.02(c)(7), but in no case may the pitcher be allowed to pitch with such attachment to his hand, finger or wrist.

(8) Intentionally delay the game by throwing the ball to players other than the catcher, when the batter is in position, except in an attempt to retire a runner.

PENALTY: If, after warning by the umpire, such delaying action is repeated, the pitcher shall be removed from the game.

(9) Intentionally Pitch at the Batter.

If, in the umpire's judgment, such a violation occurs, the umpire may elect either to:

(A) Expel the pitcher, or the manager and the pitcher, from the game, or

(B) may warn the pitcher and the manager of both teams that another such pitch will result in the immediate expulsion of that pitcher (or a replacement) and the manager.

If, in the umpire's judgment, circumstances warrant, both teams may be officially "warned" prior to the game or at any time during the game.

(The Office of the Commissioner may take additional action under authority provided in Rule 8.04.)

Rule 6.02(c)(9) Comment: Team personnel may not come onto the playing surface to argue or dispute a warning issued under Rule 6.02(c)(9). If a manager, coach or player leaves the dugout or his position to dispute a warning, he should be warned to stop. If he continues, he is subject to ejection.

To pitch at a batter's head is unsportsmanlike and highly dangerous. It should be—and is—condemned by everybody. Umpires should act without hesitation in enforcement of this rule.

(d) *PENALTY:* For violation of any part of (c)(2) through (7):

(1) The pitcher shall be ejected immediately from the game and shall be suspended automatically. In the Minor Leagues, the automatic suspension shall be for 10 games.

(2) If a play follows the violation called by the umpire, the manager of the team at bat may advise the umpire-in-chief that he elects to accept the play. Such election shall be made immediately at the end of the play. However, if the batter reaches first base on a hit, an error, a base on balls, a hit batsman, or otherwise, and no other runner is put out before advancing at least one base, the play shall proceed without reference to the violation.

(3) Even though the team at bat elects to take the play, the violation shall be recognized and the penalties in subsection 1 will still be in effect.

(4) If the manager of the team at bat does not elect to accept the play, the umpire-in-chief shall call an automatic ball or, if there are any runners on base, a balk.

(5) The umpire shall be sole judge on whether any portion of this rule has been violated.

Rule 6.02(d)(1) through 6.02(d)(5) Comment: If a pitcher violates either Rule 6.02(c)(2) or Rule 6.02(c)(3) and, in the judgment of the umpire, the pitcher did not intend, by his act, to alter the characteristics of a pitched ball, then the umpire may, in his discretion, warn the pitcher in lieu of applying the penalty set forth for violations of Rules 6.02(c)(2) through 6.02(c)(6). If the pitcher persists in violating either of those Rules, however, the umpire should then apply the penalty.

Rule 6.02(d) Comment: If at any time the ball hits the rosin bag it is in play. In the case of rain or wet field, the umpire may instruct the pitcher to carry the rosin bag in his hip pocket. A pitcher may use the rosin bag for the purpose of applying rosin to his bare hand or hands. Neither the pitcher nor any other player shall dust the ball with the rosin bag; neither shall the pitcher nor any other player be permitted to apply rosin from the bag to his glove or dust any part of his uniform with the rosin bag.

6.03 Batter Illegal Action

(a) **A batter is out for illegal action when:**

    (1) He hits a ball with one or both feet on the ground entirely outside the batter's box.

Rule 6.03(a)(1) Comment: If a batter hits a ball fair or foul while out of the batter's box, he shall be called out. Umpires should pay particular attention to the position of the batter's feet if he attempts to hit the ball while he is being intentionally passed. A batter cannot jump or step out of the batter's box and hit the ball.

    (2) He steps from one batter's box to the other while the pitcher is in position ready to pitch;

    (3) He interferes with the catcher's fielding or throwing by stepping out of the batter's box or making any other movement that hinders the catcher's play at home base.

    (4) He throws his bat into fair or foul territory and hits a catcher (including the catcher's glove) and the catcher

was attempting to catch a pitch with a runner(s) on base and/or the pitch was a third strike.

EXCEPTION to Rules 6.03(a)(3) and (4): Batter is not out if any runner attempting to advance is put out, or if runner trying to score is called out for batter's interference.

Rules 6.03(a)(3) and (4) Comment: If the batter interferes with the catcher, the plate umpire shall call "interference." The batter is out and the ball dead. No player may advance on such interference (offensive interference) and all runners must return to the last base that was, in the judgment of the umpire, legally touched at the time of the interference.

If, however, the catcher makes a play and the runner attempting to advance is put out, it is to be assumed there was no actual interference and that runner is out—not the batter. Any other runners on the base at the time may advance as the ruling is that there is no actual interference if a runner is retired. In that case play proceeds just as if no violation had been called.

If a batter strikes at a ball and misses and swings so hard he carries the bat all the way around and, in the umpire's judgment, unintentionally hits the catcher or the ball in back of him on the backswing, it shall be called a strike only (not interference). The ball will be dead, however, and no runner shall advance on the play.

(5) He uses or attempts to use a bat that, in the umpire's judgment, has been altered or tampered with in such a way to improve the distance factor or cause an unusual reaction on the baseball. This includes bats that are filled, flat-surfaced, nailed, hollowed, grooved or covered with a substance such as paraffin, wax, etc.

No advancement on the bases will be allowed (except advancements that are not caused by the use of an illegal bat, e,g., stolen base, balk, wild pitch, passed ball), and any out or outs made during a play shall stand. In addition to being called out, the player shall be ejected from the game and may be subject to additional penalties as determined by the Office of the Commissioner.

Rule 6.03(a)(5) Comment: A batter shall be deemed to have used or attempted to use an illegal bat if he brings such a bat into the batter's box.

(b) **Batting Out of Turn**

(1) A batter shall be called out, on appeal, when he fails to bat in his proper turn, and another batter completes a time at bat in his place.

(2) The proper batter may take his place in the batter's box at any time before the improper batter becomes a runner or is put out, and any balls and strikes shall be counted in the proper batter's time at bat.

(3) When an improper batter becomes a runner or is put out, and the defensive team appeals to the umpire before the first pitch to the next batter of either team, or before any play or attempted play, the umpire shall (1) declare the proper batter out; and (2) nullify any advance or score made because of a ball batted by the improper batter or because of the improper batter's advance to first base on a hit, an error, a base on balls, a hit batter or otherwise.

(4) If a runner advances, while the improper batter is at bat, on a stolen base, balk, wild pitch or passed ball, such advance is legal.

(5) When an improper batter becomes a runner or is put out, and a pitch is made to the next batter of either team before an appeal is made, the improper batter thereby becomes the proper batter, and the results of his time at bat become legal.

(6) When the proper batter is called out because he has failed to bat in turn, the next batter shall be the batter whose name follows that of the proper batter thus called out.

(7) When an improper batter becomes a proper batter because no appeal is made before the next pitch, the next batter shall be the batter whose name follows that of such legalized improper batter. The instant an improper batter's actions are legalized, the batting order picks up with the name following that of the legalized improper batter.

Rule 6.03(b)(7) Comment: The umpire shall not direct the attention of any person to the presence in the batter's box of an improper batter. This rule is designed to require constant vigilance by the players and managers of both teams.

There are two fundamentals to keep in mind: When a player bats out of turn, the proper batter is the player called out. If an improper batter bats and reaches base or is out and no appeal is made before a pitch to the next batter, or before any play or attempted play, that improper batter is considered to have batted in proper turn and establishes the order that is to follow.

APPROVED RULING: To illustrate various situations arising from batting out of turn, assume a first-inning batting order as follows:

Abel-Baker-Charles-Daniel-Edward-Frank-George-Hooker-Irwin.

PLAY (1) — Baker bats. With the count 2 balls and 1 strike, (a) the offensive team discovers the error or (b) the defensive team appeals. Ruling—In either case, Abel replaces Baker, with the count on him 2 balls and 1 strike.

PLAY (2)—Baker bats and doubles. The defensive team appeals (a) immediately or (b) after a pitch to Charles.

RULING: (a) Abel is called out and Baker is the proper batter; (b) Baker stays on second and Charles is the proper batter.

PLAY (3)—Abel walks. Baker walks. Charles forces Baker. Edward bats in Daniel's turn. While Edward is at bat, Abel scores and Charles goes to second on a wild pitch. Edward grounds out, sending Charles to third. The defensive team appeals (a) immediately or (b) after a pitch to Daniel.

RULING: (a) Abel's run counts and Charles is entitled to second base since these advances were not made because of the improper batter batting a ball or advancing to first base. Charles must return to second base because his advance to third resulted from the improper batter batting a ball. Daniel is called out, and Edward is the proper batter; (b)

Abel's run counts and Charles stays on third. The proper batter is Frank.

PLAY (4)—With the bases full and two out. Hooker bats in Frank's turn, and triples, scoring three runs. The defensive team appeals (a) immediately, or (b) after a pitch to George.

RULING: (a) Frank is called out and no runs score. George is the proper batter to lead off the second inning; (b) Hooker stays on third and three runs score. Irwin is the proper batter.

PLAY (5)—After Play (4)(b) above, George continues at bat. (a) Hooker is picked off third base for the third out, or (b) George flies out, and no appeal is made. Who is the proper leadoff batter in the second inning?

RULING: (a) Irwin. He became the proper batter as soon as the first pitch to George legalized Hooker's triple; (b) Hooker. When no appeal was made, the first pitch to the leadoff batter of the opposing team legalized George's time at bat.

PLAY (6)—Daniel walks and Abel comes to bat. Daniel was an improper batter, and if an appeal is made before the first pitch to Abel, Abel is out, Daniel is removed from base, and Baker is the proper batter. There is no appeal, and a pitch is made to Abel. Daniel's walk is now legalized, and Edward thereby becomes the proper batter. Edward can replace Abel at any time before Abel is put out or becomes a runner. He does not do so. Abel flies out, and Baker comes to bat. Abel was an improper batter, and if an appeal is made before the first pitch to Baker, Edward is out, and the proper batter is Frank. There is no appeal, and a pitch is made to Baker. Abel's out is now legalized, and the proper batter is Baker. Baker walks. Charles is the proper batter. Charles flies out. Now Daniel is the proper batter, but he is on second base. Who is the proper batter?

RULING: The proper batter is Edward. When the proper batter is on base, he is passed over, and the following batter becomes the proper batter.

6.04 Unsportsmanlike Conduct

(a) No manager, player, substitute, coach, trainer or batboy shall at any time, whether from the bench, the coach's box or on the playing field, or elsewhere:

(1) Incite, or try to incite, by word or sign a demonstration by spectators;

(2) Use language which will in any manner refer to or reflect upon opposing players, an umpire, or any spectator;

(3) Call "Time," or employ any other word or phrase or commit any act while the ball is alive and in play for the obvious purpose of trying to make the pitcher commit a balk.

(4) Make intentional contact with the umpire in any manner.

(b) Players in uniform shall not address or mingle with spectator, nor sit in the stands before, during, or after a game. No manager, coach or player shall address any spectator before or during a game. Players of opposing teams shall not fraternize at any time while in uniform.

(c) No fielder shall take a position in the batter's line of vision, and with deliberate unsportsmanlike intent, act in a manner to distract the batter.

PENALTY: The offender shall be removed from the game and shall leave the playing field, and, if a balk is made, it shall be nullified.

(d) When a manager, player, coach or trainer is ejected from a game, he shall leave the field immediately and take no further part in that game. He shall remain in the clubhouse or change to street clothes and either leave the park or take a seat in the grandstand well removed from the vicinity of his team's bench or bullpen.

Rule 6.04(d) Comment: If a manager, coach or player is under suspension he may be in uniform and may participate in the regular pre-game routines of the Club. At game time, however, suspended personnel must be out of uniform, may not be in the dugout, and must be away from areas where players are expected to be during a game. Suspended personnel also are not permitted in the press box or any broadcast areas during the course of a game, but are permitted to watch the game from the stands or suite level.

(e) When the occupants of a player's bench show violent disapproval of an umpire's decision, the umpire shall first give warning that such disapproval shall cease.

PENALTY: [If such action continues] The umpire shall order the offenders from the bench to the clubhouse. If he is unable to detect the offender, or offenders, he may clear the bench of all substitute players. The manager of the offending team shall have the privilege of recalling to the playing field only those players needed for substitution in the game.

7.00–ENDING THE GAME

7.01 Regulation Games

(a) A regulation game consists of nine innings, unless extended because of a tie score, or shortened (1) because the home team needs none of its half of the ninth inning or only a fraction of it, or (2) because the umpire-in-chief or the Office of the Commissioner calls the game.

(b) Extra Innings

(1) If the score is tied after nine completed innings, play shall continue until (1) the visiting team has scored more total runs than the home team at the end of a completed inning, or (2) the home team scores the winning run in an uncompleted inning.

(2) Each half-inning following the ninth inning will begin with a runner on second base, as follows:

(A) The batter (or a substitute for the batter) who leads off an inning shall continue to be the batter who would lead off the inning in the absence of this Extra Innings rule.

(B) The runner placed on second base at the start of each half-inning shall be the player (or a substitute for such player) in the batting order immediately preceding that half-inning's leadoff hitter. By way of example, if the number five hitter in the batting order is due to lead off the tenth inning, the number four player in the batting order (or a pinch-runner for such player) shall begin the inning on second base. However, if the player in the batting order immediately preceding that half-inning's leadoff hitter is the pitcher, the runner placed on second base at the start of that half-inning may be the player preceding the pitcher in the batting order. Any runner or batter removed from the game for a substitute shall be ineligible to return to the game in accordance with Rule 5.10.

90

(C) For purposes of calculating earned runs under Rule 9.16, the runner who begins an inning on second base pursuant to this rule shall be deemed to be a runner who has reached second base because of a fielding error, but no error shall be charged to the opposing team or to any player. For purposes of Rule 9.02, the Official Scorer shall keep records of the number of times each batter and runner is placed at second base in accordance with this rule.

(D) Starting in the tenth inning and until the game has ended, the plate umpire shall check the offensive team's line-up card to verify the proper runner starting at second base. If an improper runner is placed, the plate umpire shall inform the offensive manager immediately and have the proper runner placed at second base. If an improper runner is noticed by an umpire or either manager after play has commenced, he shall be replaced with the proper runner and all plays made will be legal, unless a batting out of order situation nullifies the advancement. There is no penalty for an improper runner before or after scoring.

(c) The umpire-in-chief or the Office of the Commissioner may postpone or call a game because of weather, field or ballpark conditions, malfunction of, or unintentional operator error in employing equipment (e.g., retractable roof, tarpaulin, etc.), air quality, a curfew, loss of electricity or lighting, local or national emergencies or disasters, government restrictions, darkness, the health and safety of fans, players, team or stadium employees, or any extraordinary circumstances that prevent the game from being played or continued safely.

(d) A called game shall be considered a regulation game, if:

(1) five innings have been completed;

(2) the home team has scored more runs in four or four and a fraction half-innings than the visiting team has scored in five completed half-innings;

(3) the home team scores one or more runs in its half of the fifth inning to tie the score.

The score of a called regulation game is the score at the time the game is called. Notwithstanding the foregoing, a called game that would otherwise qualify as a regulation game will be treated as a suspended game covered by Rule 7.02 below if the game is called when the score is tied; or if a game is called while an inning is in progress and before the inning is completed, and the visiting team has scored one or more runs to tie the game or take the lead and the home team has not retaken the lead. The Office of the Commissioner also may determine that the circumstances of a called game are so unique or extraordinary that fairness requires that the game be treated as a suspended game or treated in a different manner.

(e) The score of a regulation game is the total number of runs scored by each team at the moment the game ends, as follows:

(1) A completed regulation game ends when the visiting team completes its half of the ninth inning if the home team is ahead.

(2) A completed regulation game ends when the ninth inning is completed, if the visiting team is ahead.

(3) If the home team scores the winning run in its half of the ninth inning (or its half of an extra inning after a tie), the game ends immediately when the winning run is scored.

EXCEPTION: If the last batter in a game hits a home run out of the playing field, the batter-runner and all runners on base are permitted to score, in accordance with the base-running rules, and the game ends when the batter-runner touches home plate.

APPROVED RULING: The batter hits a home run out of the playing field to win the game in the last half of the ninth or an extra inning, but is called out for passing a preceding runner. The game ends immediately when the winning run is scored, unless there are two out and the winning run has not yet reached home plate when the runner passes another, in which case the inning is over and only those runs that scored before the runner passes another shall count.

(4) The score of a called regulation game is the total number of runs scored by each team at the moment the game ends.

7.02 Suspended Games

(a) Any postponed game or game that is called:

(1) prior to it becoming a regulation game,

(2) when the game is tied, or

(3) while an inning is in progress and before the inning is completed, and the visiting team has scored one or more runs to tie the game or take the lead and the home team has not retied the game or retaken the lead,

must be immediately scheduled to be resumed and/or played to a completed regulation game, as described in Rule 7.02(b) below.

(b) Postponed games or suspended games described in Rule 7.02(a) above must be immediately scheduled to be resumed and/or played to a completed regulation game during a scheduled series between the Clubs (i.e., preceding the next scheduled game between the two Clubs), preferably on the same grounds, or on a mutual off-day.

(c) If a postponed or suspended game cannot be scheduled to be completed during the championship season in accordance with Rule 7.02(b) above, or the available options during the season would cause undue hardship to one or both teams, the Office of the Commissioner will determine whether and when to play or resume the game, including following the completion of the championship season, by considering all relevant factors, including whether the failure to resume and/or complete the game will materially impact the postseason.

(d) If a suspended game is not resumed to completion pursuant to Rule 7.02(c) above, and it has progressed far enough to become a regulation game at the time it was called, it shall be scored as follows:

(1) the team ahead at the time the game was called shall be declared the winner; or

(2) if the score was tied at the time the game was called, the game shall be declared a "tie game."

Notwithstanding Rule 7.02(d)(1) and (2) above, if the game was called while an inning is in progress and before the inning is completed, and the visiting team has scored one or more runs either to take the lead or tie the game, and the home team has not retaken the lead or retied the game, the score upon the completion of the last full inning shall stand for purposes of this Rule 7.02.

(e) If a postponed game is not rescheduled or a suspended game is not resumed to completion pursuant to Rule 7.02(c) above, and it did not progress far enough to become a regulation game at the time it was called, it shall be declared a "No Game" and will not count as a game for any purpose.

(f) The Minor Leagues may adopt different rules for determining regulation games and how and/or whether to postpone, reschedule, call, and/or complete postponed, tied or suspended games, in the regular season or postseason.

(g) The Major Leagues have determined that Rule 7.01(b)(2) (runner on second base in Extra Innings) does not apply to any Wild Card Series, Division Series, League Championship Series or World Series games. In addition, notwithstanding anything to the contrary contained in Rule 7.01(c), 7.01(d) or 7.02(a)-(e), the Major Leagues may adopt different rules for postponing, suspending, calling, resuming, and/or completing any games, or otherwise, in any Wild Card Series, Division Series, League Championship Series, or World Series.

(h) A suspended game shall be resumed at the exact point of suspension of the original game. The completion of a suspended game is a continuation of the original game. The lineup and batting order of both teams shall be exactly the same as the lineup and batting order at the moment of suspension, subject to the rules governing substitution. Any player may be replaced by a player who had not been in the game prior to the suspension. No player removed before the suspension may be returned to the lineup.

A player who was not with the Club when the game was suspended may be used as a substitute, even if he has taken the place of a player no longer with the Club who would not have been eligible because he had been removed from the lineup before the game was suspended.

Rule 7.02(h) Comment: If immediately prior to the call of a suspended game, a pitcher has not pitched to a minimum of three consecutive batters in accordance with Rule 5.10(g), such pitcher, when the suspended game is later resumed may, but is not required to start the resumed portion of the game. However, if he does start the resumed portion of the game, he shall have to complete pitching to his first three consecutive batters in accordance with Rule 5.10(g); and, if he does not start upon resumption of the game, he will be considered as having been substituted for and may not be used again in that game.

7.03 Forfeited Games

(a) A game may be forfeited to the opposing team when a team:

(1) Fails to appear upon the field, or being upon the field, refuses to start play within five minutes after the umpire-in-chief has called "Play" at the appointed hour for beginning the game, unless such delayed appearance is, in the umpire-in-chief's judgment, unavoidable;

(2) Employs tactics palpably designed to delay or shorten the game;

(3) Refuses to continue play during a game unless the game has been suspended or terminated by the umpire-in-chief;

(4) Fails to resume play, after a suspension, within one minute after the umpire-in-chief has called "Play;"

(5) After warning by the umpire, willfully and persistently violates any rules of the game;

(6) Fails to obey within a reasonable time the umpire's order for removal of a player from the game;

(7) Fails to appear for the second game of a doubleheader within thirty minutes after the close of the first game unless the umpire-in-chief of the first game shall have extended the time of the intermission.

(b) A game shall be forfeited to the opposing team when a team is unable or refuses to place nine players on the field.

(c) A game shall be forfeited to the visiting team if, after it has been suspended, the order of the umpire to groundskeepers respecting preparation of the field for resumption of play intentionally or willfully is not complied with.

(d) If the umpire-in-chief declares a game forfeited, he shall transmit a written report to the Office of the Commissioner within 24 hours thereafter, but failure of such transmittal shall not affect the forfeiture.

7.04 Protesting Games

Protesting a game shall never be permitted, regardless of whether such complaint is based on judgment decisions by the umpire or an allegation that an umpire misapplied these rules or otherwise rendered a decision in violation of these rules.

8.00–THE UMPIRE

8.01 Umpire Qualifications and Authority

(a) The Office of the Commissioner shall appoint one or more umpires to officiate at each league championship game. The umpires shall be responsible for the conduct of the game in accordance with these official rules and for maintaining discipline and order on the playing field during the game.

(b) Each umpire is the representative of the league and of professional baseball, and is authorized and required to enforce all of these rules. Each umpire has authority to order a player, coach, manager or Club officer or employee to do or refrain from doing anything which affects the administering of these rules, and to enforce the prescribed penalties.

(c) Each umpire has authority to rule on any point not specifically covered in these rules.

(d) Each umpire has authority to disqualify any player, coach, manager or substitute for objecting to decisions or for unsportsmanlike conduct or language, and to eject such disqualified person from the playing field. If an umpire disqualifies a player while a play is in progress, the disqualification shall not take effect until no further action is possible in that play.

(e) Each umpire has authority at his discretion to eject from the playing field (1) any person whose duties permit his presence on the field, such as ground crew members, ushers, photographers, newsmen, broadcasting crew members, etc., and (2) any spectator or other person not authorized to be on the playing field.

8.02 Appeal of Umpire Decisions

(a) Any umpire's decision which involves judgment, such as, but not limited to, whether a batted ball is fair or foul, whether a pitch is a strike or a ball, or whether a runner is safe or out, is final. No player, manager, coach or substitute shall object to any such judgment decisions.

Rule 8.02(a) Comment: Players leaving their position in the field or on base, or managers or coaches leaving the bench or coaches box, to argue on BALLS AND STRIKES will not be permitted. They should be warned if they start for the plate to protest the call. If they continue, they will be ejected from the game.

(b) If there is reasonable doubt that any umpire's decision may be in conflict with the rules, the manager may appeal the decision and ask that a correct ruling be made. Such appeal shall be made only to the umpire who made the protested decision.

(c) If a decision is appealed, the umpire making the decision may ask another umpire for information before making a final decision. No umpire shall criticize, seek to reverse or interfere with another umpire's decision unless asked to do so by the umpire making it. If the umpires consult after a play and change a call that had been made, then they have the authority to take all steps that they may deem necessary, in their discretion, to eliminate the results and consequences of the earlier call that they are reversing, including placing runners where they think those runners would have been after the play, had the ultimate call been made as the initial call, disregarding interference or obstruction that may have occurred on the play; failures of runners to tag up based upon the initial call on the field; runners passing other runners or missing bases; etc., all in the discretion of the umpires. No player, manager or coach shall be permitted to argue the exercise of the umpires' discretion in resolving the play and any person so arguing shall be subject to ejection. Notwithstanding the foregoing, correction of a missed ball-strike count shall not be permitted after a pitch is thrown to a subsequent batter, or in the case of the final batter of an inning or game, after all infielders of the defensive team leave fair territory.

Rule 8.02(c) Comment: A manager is permitted to ask the umpires for an explanation of the play and how the umpires have exercised their discretion to eliminate the results and consequences of the earlier call that the umpires are reversing. Once the umpires explain the result of the play, however, no one is permitted to argue that the umpires should have exercised their discretion in a different manner.

The manager or the catcher may request the plate umpire to ask his partner for help on a half swing when the plate umpire calls the pitch a ball, but not when the pitch is called a strike. The manager may not complain that the umpire made an improper call, but only that he did not ask his partner for help. Field umpires must be alerted to the request from the plate umpire and quickly respond. Managers may not protest the call of a ball or strike on the pretense they are asking for information about a half swing.

Appeals on a half swing may be made only on the call of ball and when asked to appeal, the home plate umpire must refer to a base umpire for his judgment on the half swing. Should the base umpire call the pitch a strike, the strike call shall prevail. Appeals on a half swing must be made before the next pitch, or any play or attempted play. If the half swing occurs during a play which ends a half-inning, the appeal must be made before all infielders of the defensive team leave fair territory.

Baserunners must be alert to the possibility that the base umpire on appeal from the plate umpire may reverse the call of a ball to the call of a strike, in which event the runner is in jeopardy of being out by the catcher's throw. Also, a catcher must be alert in a base stealing situation if a ball call is reversed to a strike by the base umpire upon appeal from the plate umpire.

The ball is in play on appeal on a half swing.

On a half swing, if the manager comes out to argue with first or third base umpire and if after being warned he persists in arguing, he can be ejected as he is now arguing over a called ball or strike.

(d) No umpire may be replaced during a game unless he is injured or becomes ill.

If there is only one umpire, he shall have complete jurisdiction in administering the rules. He may take any position on the playing field which will enable him to discharge his duties (usually behind the catcher, but sometimes behind the pitcher if there are runners). He shall be considered umpire-in-chief.

(e) If there are two or more umpires, one shall be designated umpire-in-chief and the others field umpires.

8.03 Umpire Position

(a) The umpire-in-chief shall stand behind the catcher. (He usually is called the plate umpire.) His duties shall be to:

    (1) Take full charge of, and be responsible for, the proper conduct of the game;

    (2) Call and count balls and strikes;

    (3) Call and declare fair balls and fouls except those commonly called by field umpires;

    (4) Make all decisions on the batter;

    (5) Make all decisions except those commonly reserved for the field umpires;

    (6) Decide when a game shall be forfeited;

    (7) If a time limit has been set, announce the fact and the time set before the game starts;

    (8) Inform the Official Scorer of the official batting order, and any changes in the lineups and batting order, on request;

    (9) Announce any special ground rules, at his discretion.

(b) A field umpire may take any position on the playing field he thinks best suited to make impending decisions on the bases. His duties shall be to:

    (1) Make all decisions on the bases except those specifically reserved to the umpire-in-chief;

    (2) Take concurrent jurisdiction with the umpire-in-chief in calling "Time," balks, illegal pitches, or defacement or discoloration of the ball by any player.

    (3) Aid the umpire-in-chief in every manner in enforcing the rules, and excepting the power to forfeit the game, shall have equal authority with the umpire-in-chief in administering and enforcing the rules and maintaining discipline.

(c) If different decisions should be made on one play by different umpires, the umpire-in-chief shall call all the umpires into consultation, with no manager or player present. After consultation, the umpire-in-chief (unless another umpire may have been designated by the Office of the Commissioner) shall determine which decision shall prevail, based on which umpire was in best position and which decision was most likely correct. Play shall proceed as if only the final decision had been made.

8.04 Reporting

(a) The umpire shall report to the Office of the Commissioner after the end of a game all violations of rules and other incidents worthy of comment, including the disqualification of any trainer, manager, coach or player, and the reasons therefor.

(b) When any trainer, manager, coach or player is disqualified for a flagrant offense such as the use of obscene or indecent language, or an assault upon an umpire, trainer, manager, coach or player, the umpire shall forward full particulars to the Office of the Commissioner after the end of the game.

(c) After receiving the umpire's report that a trainer, manager, coach or player has been disqualified, the Office of the Commissioner shall impose such penalty as it deems justified, and shall notify the person penalized and the Club of which the penalized person is a member. If the penalty includes a fine, the penalized person shall pay the amount of the fine to the league as directed in the notice of discipline. Failure to pay such fine as directed shall result in the offender being debarred from participation in any game and from sitting on the players' bench during any game, until the fine is paid.

GENERAL INSTRUCTIONS TO UMPIRES

Umpires, on the field, should not indulge in conversation with players. Keep out of the coaching box and do not talk to the coach on duty.

Keep your uniform in good condition. Be active and alert on the field.

Be courteous, always, to Club officials; avoid visiting in Club offices and thoughtless familiarity with officers or employees of contesting Clubs.

When you enter a ball park your sole duty is to umpire a ball game as the representative of baseball.

Do not allow criticism to keep you from studying out bad situations. Carry your rule book. It is better to consult the rules and hold up the game ten minutes to decide a knotty problem than to inadvertently misapply these rules.

Keep the game moving. A ball game is often helped by energetic and earnest work of the umpires.

You are the only official representative of baseball on the ball field. It is often a trying position which requires the exercise of much patience and good judgment, but do not forget that the first essential in working out of a bad situation is to keep your own temper and self-control.

You no doubt are going to make mistakes, but never attempt to "even up" after having made one. Make all decisions as you see them and forget which is the home or visiting Club.

Keep your eye everlastingly on the ball while it is in play. It is more vital to know just where a fly ball fell, or a thrown ball finished up, than whether or not a runner missed a base. Do not call the plays too quickly, or turn away too fast when a fielder is throwing to complete a double play. Watch out for dropped balls after you have called a man out.

Do not come running with your arm up or down, denoting "out" or "safe." Wait until the play is completed before making any arm motion.

Each umpire team should work out a simple set of signals, so the proper umpire can always right a manifestly wrong decision when convinced he has made an error. If sure you got the play correctly, do not be stampeded by players' appeals to "ask the other man." If not sure, ask one of your associates. Do not carry this to extremes, be alert and get your own plays. But remember! The first requisite is to get decisions correctly. If in doubt don't hesitate to consult your associate. Umpire dignity is important but never as important as "being right."

Most important rule for umpires is always "BE IN POSITION TO SEE EVERY PLAY." Even though your decision may be 100% right, players still question it if they feel you were not in a spot to see the play clearly and definitely.

Finally, be courteous, impartial and firm, and so compel respect from all.

THE RULES OF SCORING

Index

9.00—THE OFFICIAL SCORER

9.01 Official Scorer (General Rules)

(a) The Office of the Commissioner, with respect to Major League games, and the Commissioner's designee, with respect to Minor League games, shall appoint an Official Scorer for each league championship, post-season or all-star game. The Official Scorer shall observe the game from a position in the press box, in permanent assigned seating as designated by the home Club, in a seat adjacent to league Official Data Collection staff. The Official Scorer shall have sole authority to make all decisions concerning application of Rule 9 that involve judgment, such as whether a batter's advance to first base is the result of a hit or

Rule 9.01(a)

an error. The Official Scorer shall communicate such decisions first to league Official Data Collection staff, and second to staff and media personnel in the press box and broadcasting booths by hand signals or over the press box loudspeaker system and shall advise the public address announcer of such decisions, if requested. All persons, including Club officials and players, are prohibited from protesting to the Official Scorer or league Official Data Collection staff regarding any such decisions.

The Official Scorer shall make all decisions concerning judgment calls. Upon conclusion of an event in the field requiring a scorer's judgment, the Official Scorer will first make a "preliminary" judgment call, generally using best efforts to do so in a timely fashion in line with the general pace of play, and no later than the start of the next plate appearance. Within 24 hours after a game concludes or is suspended, the Official Scorer will, at his or her discretion, render such preliminary judgments as "final," or revise the initial judgment call to become a final judgment. A Major League player or Club may request that the Commissioner's designee review a final judgment call of an Official Scorer made in a game in which such player or Club participated, by notifying the Office of the Commissioner in writing or by approved electronic means within 72 hours of a judgment becoming final. The Commissioner's designee shall have access to all relevant and available video and, after considering any evidence he wishes to consider, may order a change in a final judgment call if he determines that the final judgment of the Official Scorer was clearly erroneous. No judgment decision shall be changed thereafter. If the Commissioner's designee determines that a player or Club has abused the appeals process by repeatedly filing frivolous appeals, or acting in bad faith, he may, after providing a warning, impose reasonable sanctions on the Club or player. A Minor League player or Club may request that the Office of the Commissioner review a judgment call of an Official Scorer in accordance with league rules.

After each game, including forfeited and called games, the Official Scorer shall prepare a report, on a form prescribed by the Office of the Commissioner, with respect to Major League games, and the Commissioner's designee, with respect to

105

Minor League games, listing the date of the game, where it was played, the names of the competing Clubs and the umpires, the full score of the game and all records of individual players compiled according to the system specified in this Rule 9. The Official Scorer shall forward this report to the Office of the Commissioner, with respect to Major League and Minor League games, as soon as practicable after the game ends. The Official Scorer shall forward the report of any suspended game as soon as practicable after the game has been completed, or after it becomes a called game because it cannot be completed, as provided by the Rule 7.02.

Rule 9.01(a) Comment: The Official Scorer shall forward the official score report to the league statistician instead of to the league office, if requested to do so by the league. In the event of any discrepancy in records maintained by a league statistician and the rulings by an Official Scorer, the report of such Official Scorer shall control. League statisticians and Official Scorers should consult cooperatively to resolve any discrepancies.

(b) (1) In all cases, the Official Scorer shall not make a scoring decision that is in conflict with Rule 9 or any other Official Baseball Rule. The Official Scorer shall conform strictly to the rules of scoring set forth in this Rule 9. The Official Scorer shall not make any decision that conflicts with an umpire's decision. The Official Scorer shall have authority to rule on any point not specifically covered in these rules. The Office of the Commissioner, with respect to Major League and Minor League scorers shall order changed any decision of an Official Scorer that contradicts the rules of scoring set forth in this Rule 9 and shall take whatever remedial actions as may be necessary to correct any statistics that need correction as a result of such mistaken scoring decision.

(2) If the teams change sides before three men are put out, the Official Scorer shall immediately inform the umpire-in-chief of the mistake.

(3) If the game is suspended, the Official Scorer shall make a note of the exact situation at the time of the suspension, including the score, the number of outs, the position of any runners, the ball-and-strike count on the batter, the lineups of both teams and the players who have been removed from the game for each team.

Rule 9.01(b)(3) Comment: It is important that a suspended game resume with exactly the same situation as existed at the time of suspension.

(4) The Official Scorer shall not call the attention of any umpire or of any member of either team to the fact that a player is batting out of turn.

(c) The Official Scorer for Major League and Minor League games is an official representative who is entitled to the respect and dignity of his office and shall be accorded full protection by the Office of the Commissioner. The Official Scorer shall report to the appropriate league official any indignity expressed by any manager, player, Club employee, Club officer, or media personnel in the course of, or as the result of, the discharge of Official Scorer duties.

9.02 Official Scorer Report

The official score report prepared by the Official Scorer shall be in a form prescribed by the league and shall include:

(a) The following records for each batter and runner:

(1) Number of times batted, except that no time at bat shall be charged when a player

(A) hits a sacrifice bunt or sacrifice fly;

(B) is awarded first base on four called balls;

(C) is hit by a pitched ball; or

(D) is awarded first base because of interference or obstruction;

(2) Number of runs scored;

(3) Number of safe hits;

(4) Number of runs batted in;

(5) Two-base hits;

(6) Three-base hits;

(7) Home runs;

(8) Total bases on safe hits;

(9) Stolen bases;

(10) Sacrifice bunts;

(11) Sacrifice flies;

(12) Total number of bases on balls;

(13) Separate listing of any intentional bases on balls;

(14) Number of times hit by a pitched ball;

(15) Number of times awarded first base for interference or obstruction;

(16) Strikeouts;

(17) Number of force double plays and reverse-force double plays grounded into; and

Rule 9.02(a)(17) Comment: The Official Scorer should not charge a batter with grounding into a double play if the batter-runner is called out due to interference by a preceding runner.

(18) Number of times caught stealing.

(b) The following records for each fielder:

(1) Number of putouts;

(2) Number of assists;

(3) Number of errors;

(4) Number of double plays participated in; and

(5) Number of triple plays participated in.

(c) The following records for each pitcher:

(1) Number of innings pitched;

Rule 9.02(c)(1) Comment: In computing innings pitched, the Official Scorer shall count each putout as ⅓ of an inning. For example, if a starting pitcher is replaced with one out in the sixth inning, the Official Scorer shall credit that pitcher with 5⅓ innings. If a starting pitcher is replaced with none out in the sixth inning, the Official Scorer shall credit that pitcher with 5 innings and make the notation that that pitcher faced _____ batters in the sixth, noting the number of batters faced. If a relief pitcher retires two batters and is replaced, the Official Scorer shall credit that pitcher with ⅔ of an inning pitched. If a relief pitcher enters a game and his team initiates a successful appeal play that results in one out, the officer scorer shall credit such relief pitcher with ⅓ of an inning pitched.

    (2) Total number of batters faced;

    (3) Number of batters officially at bat against pitcher, computed according to Rule 9.02(a)(1);

    (4) Number of hits allowed;

    (5) Number of runs allowed;

    (6) Number of earned runs allowed;

    (7) Number of home runs allowed;

    (8) Number of sacrifice hits allowed;

    (9) Number of sacrifice flies allowed;

    (10) Total number of bases on balls allowed;

    (11) Separate listing of any intentional bases on balls allowed;

    (12) Number of batters hit by pitched balls;

    (13) Number of strikeouts;

    (14) Number of wild pitches; and

    (15) Number of balks.

(d) The following additional data:

    (1) Name of the winning pitcher;

(2) Name of the losing pitcher;

(3) Names of the starting pitcher and the finishing pitcher for each team; and

(4) Name of pitcher credited with a save, if any.

(e) Number of passed balls allowed by each catcher.

(f) Name of players participating in double plays and triple plays.

Rule 9.02(f) Comment: For example, an Official Scorer would note: "Double Plays—Jones, Roberts and Smith (2). Triple Play—Jones and Smith."

(g) Number of runners left on base by each team. This total shall include all runners who get on base by any means and who do not score and are not put out. The Official Scorer shall include in this total a batter-runner whose batted ball results in another runner being retired for the third out.

(h) Names of batters who hit home runs with the bases full.

(i) Number of outs when winning run scored, if the game was won in the last half-inning.

(j) The score by innings for each team.

(k) Names of umpires, listed in this order: plate umpire, first-base umpire, second-base umpire, third-base umpire, left-field umpire (if any) and right-field umpire (if any).

(l) Time required to play the game, with delays deducted for weather, light failure or technological failure not related to game action.

Rule 9.02(l) Comment: A delay to attend to the injury of a player, manager, coach or umpire shall be counted in computing time of game.

(m) Official attendance, as provided by the home Club.

9.03 Official Score Report (Additional Rules)

(a) In compiling the official score report, the Official Scorer shall list each player's name and fielding position, or positions, in the order in which the player batted, or would have batted if the game ended before the player came to bat.

Rule 9.03(a) Comment: When a player does not exchange positions with another fielder but is merely placed in a different spot for a particular batter (for example, if a second baseman goes to the outfield to form a four-man outfield, or if a third baseman moves to a position between the shortstop and second baseman), the Official Scorer should not list this as a new position.

(b) The Official Scorer shall identify in the official score report any player who enters the game as a substitute batter or substitute runner, whether or not such player continues in the game thereafter, in the batting order by a special symbol that shall refer to a separate record of substitute batters and runners. The record of substitute batters shall describe what the substitute batter did. The record of substitute batters and runners shall include the name of any such substitute whose name is announced, but who is removed for another substitute before he actually gets into the game. Any such second substitute shall be recorded as batting or running for the first announced substitute.

Rule 9.03(b) Comment: Lower case letters are recommended as symbols for substitute batters and numerals are recommended as symbols for substitute runners. For example, an official score report may note as follows: "a-Singled for Abel in third inning; b-Flied out for Baker in sixth inning; c-Hit into force for Charles in seventh inning; d-Grounded out for Daniel in ninth inning; 1-Ran for Edward in ninth inning." If a substitute's name is announced but the substitute is removed for another substitute before he actually gets into the game, the Official Scorer report shall record the substitute, for example, as follows: "e-Announced as substitute for Frank in seventh inning."

(c) How to Prove a Box Score

A box score shall balance (or is proven) when the total of the team's times at bat, bases on balls received, hit batters, sacrifice bunts, sacrifice flies and batters awarded first base because of interference or obstruction equals the total of that team's runs, players left on base and the opposing team's putouts.

(d) When Player Bats Out of Turn

When a player bats out of turn and is put out, and the proper batter is called out before the ball is pitched to the next batter, the Official Scorer shall charge the proper batter with a time at bat and score the putout and any assists the same as if the correct batting order had been followed. If an improper batter becomes a runner and the proper batter is called out for having missed his turn at bat, the Official Scorer shall charge the proper batter with a time at bat, credit the putout to the catcher and ignore everything entering into the improper batter's safe arrival on base. If more than one batter bats out of turn in succession, the Official Scorer shall score all plays just as they occur, skipping the turn at bat of the player or players who first missed batting in the proper order.

(e) Called and Forfeited Games

(1) If a regulation game is called, the Official Scorer shall include the record of all individual and team actions up to the moment the game ends, as defined in Rule 7.01. If the game is a tie game, the Official Scorer shall not enter a winning or losing pitcher.

(2) If a regulation game is forfeited, the Official Scorer shall include the record of all individual and team actions up to the time of forfeit. If the winning team by forfeit is ahead at the time of forfeit, the Official Scorer shall enter as winning and losing pitchers the players who would have qualified as the winning and losing pitchers if the game had been called at the time of forfeit. If the winning team by forfeit is behind or if the score is tied at the time of forfeit, the Official Scorer shall not enter a winning or losing pitcher. If a game is forfeited before it becomes a regulation game, the Official Scorer shall include no records and shall report only the fact of the forfeit.

Rule 9.03(e) Comment: The Official Scorer shall not consider that, by rule, the score of a forfeited game is 9 to 0 (*see* Definition of Terms (Forfeited Game)), notwithstanding the results on the field at the point the game is forfeited.

9.04 Runs Batted In

A run batted in is a statistic credited to a batter whose action at bat causes one or more runs to score, as set forth in this Rule 9.04.

(a) The Official Scorer shall credit the batter with a run batted in for every run that scores

    (1) unaided by an error and as part of a play begun by the batter's safe hit (including the batter's home run), sacrifice bunt, sacrifice fly, infield out or fielder's choice, unless Rule 9.04(b) applies;

    (2) by reason of the batter becoming a runner with the bases full (because of a base on balls, an award of first base for being touched by a pitched ball or for interference or obstruction); or

    (3) when, before two are out, an error is made on a play on which a runner from third base ordinarily would score.

(b) The Official Scorer shall not credit a run batted in

    (1) when the batter grounds into a force double play or a reverse-force double play; or

    (2) when a fielder is charged with an error because the fielder muffs a throw at first base that would have completed a force double play.

(c) The Official Scorer's judgment must determine whether a run batted in shall be credited for a run that scores when a fielder holds the ball or throws to a wrong base. Ordinarily, if the runner keeps going, the Official Scorer should credit a run batted in; if the runner stops and takes off again when the runner notices the misplay, the Official Scorer should credit the run as scored on a fielder's choice.

9.05 Base Hits

A base hit is a statistic credited to a batter when such batter reaches base safely, as set forth in this Rule 9.05.

(a) The Official Scorer shall credit a batter with a base hit when:

    (1) the batter reaches first base (or any succeeding base)

safely on a fair ball that settles on the ground, that touches a fence before being touched by a fielder or that clears a fence;

(2) the batter reaches first base safely on a fair ball hit with such force, or so slowly, that any fielder attempting to make a play with the ball has no opportunity to do so;

Rule 9.05(a)(2) Comment: The Official Scorer shall credit a hit if the fielder attempting to handle the ball cannot make a play, even if such fielder deflects the ball from or cuts off another fielder who could have put out a runner.

(3) the batter reaches first base safely on a fair ball that takes an unnatural bounce so that a fielder cannot handle it with ordinary effort, or that touches the pitcher's plate or any base (including home plate) before being touched by a fielder and bounces so that a fielder cannot handle the ball with ordinary effort;

(4) the batter reaches first base safely on a fair ball that has not been touched by a fielder and that is in fair territory when the ball reaches the outfield, unless in the scorer's judgment the ball could have been handled with ordinary effort;

(5) a fair ball that has not been touched by a fielder touches a runner or an umpire, unless a runner is called out for having been touched by an Infield Fly, in which case the Official Scorer shall not score a hit; or

(6) a fielder unsuccessfully attempts to put out a preceding runner and, in the Official Scorer's judgment, the batter-runner would not have been put out at first base by ordinary effort.

Rule 9.05(a) Comment: In applying Rule 9.05(a), the Official Scorer shall always give the batter the benefit of the doubt. A safe course for the Official Scorer to follow is to score a hit when exceptionally good fielding of a ball fails to result in a putout.

(b) The Official Scorer shall not credit a base hit when a:

(1) runner is forced out by a batted ball, or would have been forced out except for a fielding error;

(2) batter apparently hits safely and a runner who is forced to advance by reason of the batter becoming a runner fails to touch the first base to which such runner is advancing and is called out on appeal. The Official Scorer shall charge the batter with a time at bat but no hit;

(3) pitcher, the catcher or any infielder handles a batted ball and puts out a preceding runner who is attempting to advance one base or to return to his original base, or would have put out such runner with ordinary effort except for a fielding error. The Official Scorer shall charge the batter with a time at bat but no hit;

(4) fielder fails in an attempt to put out a preceding runner and, in the scorer's judgment, the batter-runner could have been put out at first base; or

Rule 9.05(b) Comment: Rule 9.05(b) shall not apply if the fielder merely looks toward or feints toward another base before attempting to make the putout at first base.

(5) is called out for interference with a fielder attempting to field a batted ball, unless in the scorer's judgment the batter-runner would have been safe had the interference not occurred.

9.06 Determining Value of Base Hits

The Official Scorer shall score a base hit as a one-base hit, two-base hit, three-base hit or home run when no error or putout results, as follows:

(a) Subject to the provisions of Rule 9.06(b) and 9.06(c), it is a one-base hit if the batter stops at first base; it is a two-base hit if the batter stops at second base; it a three-base hit if the batter stops at third base; and it is a home run if the batter touches all bases and scores.

(b) When, with one or more runners on base, the batter advances more than one base on a safe hit and the defensive team makes an attempt to put out a preceding runner, the scorer shall determine whether the batter made a legitimate two-base hit or three-base hit, or whether the batter-runner advanced beyond first base on the fielder's choice.

Rule 9.06 Comment: The Official Scorer shall not credit the batter with a three-base hit when a preceding runner is put out at home plate, or would have been out but for an error. The Official Scorer shall not credit the batter with a two-base hit when a preceding runner trying to advance from first base is put out at third base, or would have been out but for an error. The Official Scorer shall not, however, with the exception of the above, determine the value of base-hits by the number of bases advanced by a preceding runner. A batter may deserve a two-base hit even though a preceding runner advances one or no bases; a batter may deserve only a one-base hit even though he reaches second base and a preceding runner advances two bases. For example:

(1) Runner on first. Batter hits to right fielder, who throws to third base in an unsuccessful attempt to put out runner. Batter takes second base. The Official Scorer shall credit batter with one-base hit.

(2) Runner on second. Batter hits fair fly ball. Runner holds up to determine if ball is caught and then advances only to third base, while batter takes second base. The Official Scorer shall credit batter with two-base hit.

(3) Runner on third. Batter hits high, fair fly. Runner takes a lead, then runs back to tag up, thinking the ball will be caught. The ball falls safe, but runner cannot score, although batter has reached second. The Official Scorer shall credit batter with a two-base hit.

(c) When the batter attempts to make a two-base hit or a three-base hit by sliding, he must hold the last base to which he advances. If a batter-runner overslides and is tagged out before getting back to the base safely, he shall credit with only as many bases as he attained safely. If a batter-runner overslides second base and is tagged out, the Official Scorer shall credit him with a one-base hit; if the batter-runner overslides third base and is tagged out, the Official Scorer shall credit him with a two-base hit.

Rule 9.06(c) Comment: If the batter-runner overruns second or third base and is tagged out trying to return, the Official Scorer shall credit the batter-runner with the last base he touched. If a batter-runner runs past second base after reaching that base on his feet, attempts to return and is tagged out, the Official Scorer shall credit the batter with a two-base hit. If a batter-runner runs past third base after reaching that base on his feet, attempts to return and is tagged out, the Official Scorer shall credit the batter with a three-base hit.

(d) When the batter, after making a safe hit, is called out for having failed to touch a base, the last base the batter reached safely shall determine if the Official Scorer shall credit him with a one-base hit, a two-base hit or a three-base hit. If a batter-runner is called out after missing home plate, the Official Scorer shall credit him with a three-base hit. If a batter-runner is called out for missing third base, the Official Scorer shall credit him with a two-base hit. If a batter-runner is called out for missing second base, the Official Scorer shall credit him with a one-base hit. If a batter-runner is called out for missing first base, the Official Scorer shall charge him with a time at bat, but no hit.

(e) When a batter-runner is awarded two bases, three bases or a home run under the provisions of Rules 5.06(b)(4) or 6.01(h), the Official Scorer shall credit the batter-runner with a two-base hit, a three-base hit or a home run, as the case may be.

(f) Subject to the provisions of Rule 9.06(g), when a batter ends a game with a safe hit that drives in as many runs as are necessary to put his team in the lead, the Official Scorer shall credit such batter with only as many bases on his hit as are advanced by the runner who scores the winning run, and then only if the batter runs out his hit for as many bases as are advanced by the runner who scores the winning run.

Rule 9.06(f) Comment: The Official Scorer shall apply this rule even when the batter is theoretically entitled to more bases because of being awarded an "automatic" extra-base hit under various provisions of Rules 5.05 and 5.06(b)(4).

The Official Scorer shall credit the batter with a base touched in the natural course of play, even if the winning run has scored moments before on the same play. For example, the score is tied in the bottom of the ninth inning with a runner on second base and the batter hits a ball to the outfield that falls for a base hit. The runner scores after the batter has touched first base and continued on to second base but shortly before the batter-runner reaches second base. If the batter-runner reaches second base, the Official Scorer shall credit the batter with a two-base hit.

(g) When the batter ends a game with a home run hit out of the playing field, the batter and any runners on base are entitled to score.

9.07 Stolen Bases and Caught Stealing

The Official Scorer shall credit a stolen base to a runner whenever the runner advances one base unaided by a hit, a putout, an error, a force-out, a fielder's choice, a passed ball, a wild pitch or a balk, subject to the following:

(a) When a runner starts for the next base before the pitcher delivers the ball and the pitch results in what ordinarily is scored a wild pitch or passed ball, the Official Scorer shall credit the runner with a stolen base and shall not charge the misplay, unless, as a result of the misplay, the stealing runner advances an extra base, or another runner also advances, in which case the Official Scorer shall score the wild pitch or passed ball as well as the stolen base.

(b) When a runner is attempting to steal, and the catcher, after receiving the pitch, makes a wild throw trying to prevent the stolen base, the Official Scorer shall credit the runner with a stolen base. The Official Scorer shall not charge an error unless the wild throw permits the stealing runner to advance one or more extra bases, or permits another runner to advance, in which case the Official Scorer shall credit the runner with the stolen base and charge one error to the catcher.

(c) When a runner, attempting to steal, or after being picked off base, evades being put out in a run-down play and advances to the next base without the aid of an error, the Official Scorer shall credit the runner with a stolen base. If another runner also advances on the play, the Official Scorer shall credit both runners with stolen bases. If a runner advances while another runner, attempting to steal, evades being put out in a run-down play and returns safely, without the aid of an error, to the base he originally occupied, the Official Scorer shall credit a stolen base to the runner who advances.

(d) When a double- or triple-steal is attempted and one runner is thrown out before reaching and holding the base such runner is attempting to steal, no other runner shall be credited with a stolen base.

(e) When a runner is tagged out after oversliding a base, while attempting either to return to that base or to advance to the next base, the Official Scorer shall not credit such runner with a stolen base.

(f) When in the scorer's judgment a runner attempting to steal is safe because of a muffed throw, the Official Scorer shall not credit a stolen base. The Official Scorer shall credit an assist to the fielder who made the throw, charge an error to the fielder who muffed the throw and charge the runner with "caught stealing."

(g) The Official Scorer shall not score a stolen base when a runner advances solely because of the defensive team's indifference to the runner's advance. The Official Scorer shall score such a play as a fielder's choice.

Rule 9.07(g) Comment: The scorer shall consider, in judging whether the defensive team has been indifferent to a runner's advance, the totality of the circumstances, including the inning and score of the game, whether the defensive team had held the runner on base, whether the pitcher had made any pickoff attempts on that runner before the runner's advance, whether the fielder ordinarily expected to cover the base to which the runner advanced made a move to cover such base, whether the defensive team had a legitimate strategic motive to not contest the runner's advance or whether the defensive team might be trying impermissibly to deny the runner credit for a stolen base. For example, with runners on first and third bases, the Official Scorer should ordinarily credit a stolen base when the runner on first advances to second, if, in the scorer's judgment, the defensive team had a legitimate strategic motive—namely, preventing the runner on third base from scoring on the throw to second base—not to contest the runner's advance to second base. The Official Scorer may conclude that the defensive team is impermissibly trying to deny a runner credit for a stolen base if, for example, the defensive team fails to defend the advance of a runner approaching a league or career record or a league statistical title.

(h) The Official Scorer shall charge a runner as "caught stealing" if such runner is put out, or would have been put out by errorless play, when such runner

(1) tries to steal;

(2) is picked off a base and tries to advance (any move toward the next base shall be considered an attempt to advance); or

(3) overslides while stealing.

Rule 9.07(h) Comment: In those instances where a pitched ball eludes the catcher and the runner is put out trying to advance, the Official Scorer shall not charge any "caught stealing." The Official Scorer shall not charge any caught stealing when a runner is awarded a base due to obstruction or when a runner is called out due to interference by the batter. The Official Scorer shall not charge a runner with a caught stealing if such runner would not have been credited with a stolen base had such runner been safe (for example, when a catcher throws the runner out after such runner tries to advance after a ball that had eluded the catcher on a pitch).

9.08 Sacrifices

The Official Scorer shall:

(a) Score a sacrifice bunt when, before two are out, the batter advances one or more runners with a bunt and is put out at first base, or would have been put out except for a fielding error, unless, in the judgment of the Official Scorer, the batter was bunting exclusively for a base hit and not sacrificing his own chance of reaching first base for the purpose of advancing a runner or runners, in which case the Official Scorer shall charge the batter with a time at bat;

Rule 9.08(a) Comment: In determining whether the batter had been sacrificing his own chance of reaching first base for the purpose of advancing a runner, the Official Scorer shall give the batter the benefit of the doubt. The Official Scorer shall consider the totality of the circumstances of the at-bat, including the inning, the number of outs and the score.

(b) Score a sacrifice bunt when, before two are out, the fielders handle a bunted ball without error in an unsuccessful attempt to put out a preceding runner advancing one base, unless, an attempt to turn a bunt into a putout of a preceding runner fails, and in the judgment of the Official Scorer ordinary effort would not have put out the batter at first base, in which case the batter shall be credited with a one-base hit and not a sacrifice;

(c) Not score a sacrifice bunt when any runner is put out attempting to advance one base on a bunt, or would have been put out, except for a fielding error, in which case the Official Scorer shall charge the batter with a time at bat; and

(d) Score a sacrifice fly when, before two are out, the batter hits a ball in flight handled by an outfielder or an infielder running in the outfield in fair or foul territory that

(1) is caught, and a runner scores after the catch, or

(2) is dropped, and a runner scores, if in the scorer's judgment the runner could have scored after the catch had the fly been caught.

Rule 9.08(d) Comment: The Official Scorer shall score a sacrifice fly in accordance with Rule 9.08(d)(2) even though another runner is forced out by reason of the batter becoming a runner.

9.09 Putouts

A putout is a statistic credited to a fielder whose action causes the out of a batter-runner or runner, as set forth in this Rule 9.09.

(a) The Official Scorer shall credit a putout to each fielder who

    (1) catches a ball that is in flight, whether fair or foul;

    (2) catches a batted or thrown ball and tags a base to put out a batter or runner; or

Rule 9.09(a)(2) Comment: The Official Scorer shall credit a fielder with a putout if such fielder catches a thrown ball and tags a base to record an out on an appeal play.

    (3) tags a runner when the runner is off the base to which the runner is entitled.

(b) The Official Scorer shall credit an automatic putout to the catcher when a:

    (1) batter is called out on strikes;

    (2) batter is called out for an illegally batted ball;

    (3) batter is called out for bunting foul for his third strike;

Rule 9.09(b)(3) Comment: Note the exception in Rule 9.15(a)(4).

    (4) batter is called out for being touched by his own batted ball;

    (5) batter is called out for interfering with the catcher;

    (6) batter is called out for failing to bat in his proper turn;

Rule 9.09(b)(6) Comment: See Rule 9.03(d).

    (7) batter is called out for refusing to touch first base after receiving a base on balls, after being hit by a pitch or after a catcher's interference; or

    (8) runner is called out for refusing to advance from third base to home plate.

(c) The Official Scorer shall credit automatic putouts as follows (and shall credit no assists on these plays except as specified):

(1) When the batter is called out on an Infield Fly that is not caught, the Official Scorer shall credit the putout to the fielder who the scorer believes could have made the catch;

(2) When a runner is called out for being touched by a fair ball (including an Infield Fly), the Official Scorer shall credit the putout to the fielder nearest the ball;

(3) When a runner is called out for running out of line to avoid being tagged, the Official Scorer shall credit the putout to the fielder whom the runner avoided;

(4) When a runner is called out for passing another runner, the Official Scorer shall credit the putout to the fielder nearest the point of passing;

(5) When a runner is called out for running the bases in reverse order, the Official Scorer shall credit the putout to the fielder covering the base the runner left in starting his reverse run;

(6) When a runner is called out for having interfered with a fielder, the Official Scorer shall credit the putout to the fielder with whom the runner interfered, unless the fielder was in the act of throwing the ball when the interference occurred, in which case the Official Scorer shall credit the putout to the fielder for whom the throw was intended and shall credit an assist to the fielder whose throw was interfered with; or

(7) When the batter-runner is called out because of interference by a preceding runner, as provided in Rule 6.01(a)(5), the Official Scorer shall credit the putout to the first baseman. If the fielder interfered with was in the act of throwing the ball, the Official Scorer shall credit such fielder with an assist but shall credit only one assist on any one play under the provisions of Rules 9.09(c)(6) and 9.09(c)(7).

9.10 Assists

An assist is a statistic credited to a fielder whose action contributes to a batter-runner or runner being put out, as set forth in this Rule 9.10.

(a) The Official Scorer shall credit an assist to each fielder who

    (1) throws or deflects a batted or thrown ball in such a way that a putout results, or would have resulted except for a subsequent error by any fielder. Only one assist and no more shall be credited to each fielder who throws or deflects the ball in a run-down play that results in a putout, or would have resulted in a putout, except for a subsequent error; or

Rule 9.10(a)(1) Comment: Mere ineffective contact with the ball shall not be considered an assist. "Deflect" shall mean to slow down or change the direction of the ball and thereby effectively assist in putting out a batter or runner. If a putout results from an appeal play within the natural course of play, the Official Scorer shall give assists to each fielder, except the fielder making the putout, whose action led to the putout. If a putout results from an appeal play initiated by the pitcher throwing to a fielder after the previous play has ended, the Official Scorer shall credit the pitcher, and only the pitcher, with an assist.

    (2) throws or deflects the ball during a play that results in a runner being called out for interference or for running out of line.

(b) The Official Scorer shall not credit an assist to

    (1) the pitcher on a strikeout, unless the pitcher fields an uncaught third strike and makes a throw that results in a putout;

    (2) the pitcher when, as the result of a legal pitch received by the catcher, a runner is put out, as when the catcher picks a runner off base, throws out a runner trying to steal or tags a runner trying to score; or

    (3) a fielder whose wild throw permits a runner to advance, even though the runner subsequently is put out as a result

of continuous play. A play that follows a misplay (whether or not the misplay is an error) is a new play, and the fielder making any misplay shall not be credited with an assist unless such fielder takes part in the new play.

9.11 Double and Triple Plays

The Official Scorer shall credit participation in a double play or triple play to each fielder who earns a putout or an assist when two or three players are put out between the time a pitch is delivered and the time the ball next becomes dead or is next in possession of the pitcher in a pitching position, unless an error or misplay intervenes between putouts.

Rule 9.11 Comment: The Official Scorer shall credit a double play or triple play also if an appeal play after the ball is in possession of the pitcher results in an additional putout.

9.12 Errors

An error is a statistic charged against a fielder whose action has assisted the team on offense, as set forth in this Rule 9.12.

(a) The Official Scorer shall charge an error against any fielder:

(1) whose misplay (fumble, muff or wild throw) prolongs the time at bat of a batter, prolongs the presence on the bases of a runner or permits a runner to advance one or more bases, unless, in the judgment of the Official Scorer, such fielder deliberately permits a foul fly to fall safe with a runner on third base before two are out in order that the runner on third shall not score after the catch;

Rule 9.12(a)(1) Comment: Slow handling of the ball that does not involve mechanical misplay shall not be construed as an error. For example, the Official Scorer shall not charge a fielder with an error if such fielder fields a ground ball cleanly but does not throw to first base in time to retire the batter. It is not necessary that the fielder touch the ball to be charged with an error. If a ground ball goes through a fielder's legs or a fly ball falls untouched and, in the scorer's judgment, the fielder could have handled the ball with ordinary effort, the Official Scorer shall charge such fielder with an error. For example, the Official Scorer shall charge an infielder with an error when a ground ball passes to either side of such infielder if, in the Official Scorer's judgment, a fielder at that position making ordinary effort would have fielded such ground ball and retired a runner. The Official Scorer shall charge an outfielder with an error if such outfielder allows a fly ball to drop to the ground if, in the Official Scorer's judgment, an outfielder at that position making ordinary effort would have caught such fly ball. If a throw is low, wide or high, or strikes the ground, and a runner reaches base who otherwise would have been put out by such throw, the Official Scorer shall charge the player making the throw with an error.

The Official Scorer shall not score mental mistakes or misjudgments as errors unless a specific rule prescribes otherwise. A fielder's mental mistake that leads to a physical misplay—such as throwing the ball into the stands or rolling the ball to the pitcher's mound, mistakenly believing there to be three outs, and thereby allowing a runner or runners to advance—shall not be considered a mental mistake for purposes of this rule and the Official Scorer shall charge a fielder committing such a mistake with an error. The Official Scorer shall not charge an error if the pitcher fails to cover first base on a play, thereby allowing a batter-runner to reach first base safely. The Official Scorer shall not charge an error to a fielder who incorrectly throws to the wrong base on a play.

The Official Scorer shall charge an error to a fielder who causes another fielder to misplay a ball—for example, by knocking the ball out of the other fielder's glove. On such a play, when the Official Scorer charges an error to the interfering fielder, the Official Scorer shall not charge an error to the fielder with whom the other fielder interfered.

(2) when such fielder muffs a foul fly to prolong the time at bat of a batter, whether the batter subsequently reaches first base or is put out;

(3) when such fielder catches a thrown ball or a ground ball in time to put out the batter-runner and fails to tag first base or the batter-runner;

(4) when such fielder catches a thrown ball or a ground ball in time to put out any runner on a force play and fails to tag the base or the runner;

(5) whose wild throw permits a runner to reach a base safely, when in the scorer's judgment a good throw would have put out the runner, unless such wild throw is made attempting to prevent a stolen base;

(6) whose wild throw in attempting to prevent a runner's advance permits that runner or any other runner to advance one or more bases beyond the base such runner would have reached had the throw not been wild;

(7) whose throw takes an unnatural bounce, touches a base or the pitcher's plate, or touches a runner, a fielder or an umpire, thereby permitting any runner to advance; or

Rule 9.12(a)(7) Comment: The Official Scorer shall apply this rule even when it appears to be an injustice to a fielder whose throw was accurate. For example, the Official Scorer shall charge an error to an outfielder whose accurate throw to second base hits the base and caroms back into the outfield, thereby permitting a runner or runners to advance, because every base advanced by a runner must be accounted for.

(8) whose failure to stop, or try to stop, an accurately thrown ball permits a runner to advance, so long as there was occasion for the throw. If such throw was made to second base, the Official Scorer shall determine whether it was the duty of the second baseman or the shortstop to stop the ball and shall charge an error to the negligent fielder.

Rule 9.12(a)(8) Comment: If, in the Official Scorer's judgment, there was no occasion for the throw, the Official Scorer shall charge an error to the fielder who threw the ball.

(b) The Official Scorer shall charge only one error on any wild throw, regardless of the number of bases advanced by one or more runners.

(c) When an umpire awards the batter or any runner or runners one or more bases because of interference or obstruction, the Official Scorer shall charge the fielder who committed the interference or obstruction with one error, no matter how many bases the batter, or runner or runners, may advance.

Rule 9.12(c) Comment: The Official Scorer shall not charge an error if obstruction does not change the play, in the opinion of the scorer.

(d) The Official Scorer shall not charge an error against:

  (1) the catcher when the catcher, after receiving the pitch, makes a wild throw attempting to prevent a stolen base, unless the wild throw permits the stealing runner to advance one or more extra bases or permits any other runner to advance one or more bases;

  (2) any fielder who makes a wild throw if in the scorer's judgment the runner would not have been put out with ordinary effort by a good throw, unless such wild throw permits any runner to advance beyond the base he would have reached had the throw not been wild;

  (3) any fielder who makes a wild throw in attempting to complete a double play or triple play, unless such wild throw enables any runner to advance beyond the base such runner would have reached had the throw not been wild;

Rule 9.12(d) Comment: When a fielder muffs a thrown ball that, if held, would have completed a double play or triple play, the Official Scorer shall charge an error to the fielder who drops the ball and credit an assist to the fielder who made the throw.

  (4) any fielder when, after a ground ball or dropping a batted ball that is in flight or a thrown ball, the fielder recovers the ball in time to force out a runner at any base; or

  (5) any fielder when a wild pitch or passed ball is scored.

(e) The Official Scorer shall not charge an error when the batter is awarded first base on four called balls, when the batter is awarded first base when touched by a pitched ball, or when the batter reaches first base as the result of a wild pitch or passed ball.

Rule 9.12(e) Comment: See Rule 9.13 for additional scoring rules relating to wild pitches and passed balls.

(f) The Official Scorer shall not charge an error when a runner or runners advance as the result of a passed ball, a wild pitch or a balk.

  (1) When the fourth called ball is a wild pitch or a passed ball and as a result

    (A) the batter-runner advances to a base beyond first base;

    (B) any runner forced to advance by the base on balls advances more than one base; or

    (C) any runner, not forced to advance, advances one or more bases, the Official Scorer shall score the base on balls and also the wild pitch or passed ball, as the case may be.

  (2) When the catcher recovers the ball after a wild pitch or passed ball on the third strike, and throws out the batter-runner at first base, or tags out the batter-runner, but another runner or runners advance, the Official Scorer shall score the strikeout, the putout and assists, if any, and credit the advance of the other runner or runners on the play as a fielder's choice.

Rule 9.12(f) Comment: See Rule 9.13 for additional scoring rules relating to wild pitches and passed balls.

9.13 Wild Pitches and Passed Balls

A wild pitch is defined in the Definition of Terms (Wild Pitch). A passed ball is a statistic charged against a catcher whose action has caused a runner or runners to advance, as set forth in this Rule 9.13.

(a) The Official Scorer shall charge a pitcher with a wild pitch when a legally delivered ball is so high, so wide or so low that the catcher does not stop and control the ball by ordinary effort, thereby permitting a runner or runners to advance. The Official

Scorer shall charge a pitcher with a wild pitch when a legally delivered ball touches the ground or home plate before reaching the catcher and is not handled by the catcher, thereby permitting a runner or runners to advance. When the third strike is a wild pitch, permitting the batter to reach first base, the Official Scorer shall score a strikeout and a wild pitch.

(b) The Official Scorer shall charge a catcher with a passed ball when the catcher fails to hold or to control a legally pitched ball that should have been held or controlled with ordinary effort, thereby permitting a runner or runners to advance. When the third strike is a passed ball, permitting the batter to reach first base, the Official Scorer shall score a strikeout and a passed ball.

Rule 9.13 Comment: The Official Scorer shall not charge a wild pitch or passed ball if the defensive team makes an out before any runners advance. For example, if a pitch touches the ground and eludes the catcher with a runner on first base, but the catcher recovers the ball and throws to second base in time to retire the runner, the Official Scorer shall not charge the pitcher with a wild pitch. The Official Scorer shall credit the advancement of any other runner on the play as a fielder's choice. If a catcher drops a pitch, for example, with a runner on first base, but the catcher recovers the ball and throws to second base in time to retire the runner, the Official Scorer shall not charge the catcher with a passed ball. The Official Scorer shall credit the advancement of any other runner on the play as a fielder's choice.

See Rules 9.07(a), 9.12(e) and 9.12(f) for additional scoring rules relating to wild pitches and passed balls.

9.14 Base on Balls

A base on balls is defined in the Definition of Terms (Base on Balls).

(a) The Official Scorer shall score a base on balls whenever a batter is awarded first base because of four balls having been pitched outside the strike zone, but when the fourth such ball touches the batter it shall be scored as a "hit batter."

(b) The Official Scorer shall score an intentional base on balls when the pitcher makes no attempt to throw the last pitch to the batter into the strike zone, but purposely throws the ball wide to the catcher outside the catcher's box.

(c) If a batter awarded a base on balls is called out for refusing to advance to first base, the Official Scorer shall not credit the base on balls and shall charge a time at bat.

(d) The Official Scorer shall score an intentional base on balls when a batter is awarded first base because the defensive team's manager informs the umpire of the team's intention to walk the batter.

9.15 Strikeouts

A strikeout is a statistic credited to a pitcher and charged to a batter when the umpire calls three strikes on a batter, as set forth in this Rule 9.15.

(a) The Official Scorer shall score a strikeout whenever a batter:

(1) is put out by a third strike caught by the catcher;

(2) is put out by a third strike not caught when there is a runner on first before two are out;

(3) becomes a runner because a third strike is not caught; or

(4) bunts foul on third strike, unless such bunt on third strike results in a foul fly caught by any fielder, in which case the Official Scorer shall not score a strikeout and shall credit the fielder who catches such foul fly with a putout.

(b) When a batter leaves the game with two strikes against him, and the substitute batter completes a strikeout, the Official Scorer shall charge the strikeout and the time at bat to the first batter. If the substitute batter completes the turn at bat in any other manner, including a base on balls, the Official Scorer shall score the action as having been that of the substitute batter.

Rule 9.16 to 9.16(a)

9.16 Earned Runs and Runs Allowed

An earned run is a run for which a pitcher is held accountable. In determining earned runs, the Official Scorer shall reconstruct the inning without the errors (which exclude catcher's interference) and passed balls, giving the benefit of the doubt always to the pitcher in determining which bases would have been reached by runners had there been errorless play. For the purpose of determining earned runs, an intentional base on balls, regardless of the circumstances, shall be construed in exactly the same manner as any other base on balls.

(a) The Official Scorer shall charge an earned run against a pitcher every time a runner reaches home base by the aid of safe hits, sacrifice bunts, a sacrifice fly, stolen bases, putouts, fielder's choices, bases on balls, hit batters, balks or wild pitches (including a wild pitch on third strike that permits a batter to reach first base) before fielding chances have been offered to put out the offensive team. For the purpose of this rule, a defensive interference penalty shall be construed as a fielding chance. A wild pitch is solely the pitcher's fault and shall contribute to an earned run just as a base on balls or a balk.

Rule 9.16(a) Comment: The following are examples of earned runs charged to a pitcher:

(1) Peter pitches and retires Abel and Baker, the first two batters of an inning. Charlie reaches first base on an error charged to a fielder. Daniel hits a home run. Edward hits a home run. Peter retires Frank to end the inning. Three runs have scored, but no earned runs are charged to Peter, because Charlie should have been the third out of the inning, as reconstructed without the error.

(2) Peter pitches and retires Abel. Baker hits a triple. While pitching to Charlie, Peter throws a wild pitch, allowing Baker to score. Peter retires Daniel and Edward. One run has scored, charged as an earned run to Peter, because the wild pitch contributes to an earned run.

In an inning in which a batter-runner reaches first base on a catcher's interference, such batter-runner shall

132

not count as an earned run should he subsequently score. The Official Scorer shall not assume, however, that such batter would have made an out absent the catcher's interference (unlike, for example, situations in which a batter-runner reaches first base safely because of a fielder's misplay of a ball for an error). Because such batter never had a chance to complete his time at bat, it is unknown how such batter would have fared absent the catcher's interference. Compare the following examples:

(3) With two out, Abel reaches first on an error by the shortstop in misplaying a ground ball. Baker hits a home run. Charlie strikes out. Two runs have scored, but none is earned, because Abel's at-bat should have been the third out of the inning, as reconstructed without the error.

(4) With two out, Abel reaches first on a catcher's interference. Baker hits a home run. Charlie strikes out. Two runs have scored, but one (Baker's) is earned, because the Official Scorer cannot assume that Abel would have made an out to end the inning, absent the catcher's interference.

(b) No run shall be earned when scored by a runner who reaches first base

    (1) on a hit or otherwise after his time at bat is prolonged by a muffed foul fly;

    (2) because of interference or obstruction; or

    (3) because of any fielding error.

(c) No run shall be earned when scored by a runner whose presence on the bases is prolonged by an error, if such runner would have been put out by errorless play.

(d) No run shall be earned when the scoring runner's advance has been aided by an error, a passed ball or defensive interference or obstruction, if in the Official Scorer's judgment the run would not have scored without the aid of such misplay.

(e) An error by a pitcher is treated exactly the same as an error by any other fielder in computing earned runs.

(f) Whenever a fielding error occurs, the pitcher shall be given the benefit of the doubt in determining to which bases any runners would have advanced had the fielding of the defensive team been errorless.

(g) When pitchers are changed during an inning, the Official Scorer shall not charge the relief pitcher with any run (earned or unearned) scored by a runner who was on base at the time such relief pitcher entered the game, nor for runs scored by any runner who reaches base on a fielder's choice that puts out a runner left on base by any preceding pitcher.

Rule 9.16(g) Comment: It is the intent of Rule 9.16(g) to charge each pitcher with the number of runners he put on base, rather than with the individual runners. When a pitcher puts runners on base and is relieved, such pitcher shall be charged with all runs subsequently scored up to and including the number of runners such pitcher left on base when such pitcher left the game, unless such runners are put out without action by the batter (i.e., caught stealing, picked off base or called out for interference when a batter-runner does not reach first base on the play). For example:

(1) Peter is pitching. Abel reaches first base on a base on balls. Roger relieves Peter. Baker grounds out, advancing Abel to second base. Charlie flies out. Daniel singles, scoring Abel. Abel's run is charged to Peter.

(2) Peter is pitching. Abel reaches first base on a base on balls. Roger relieves Peter. Baker forces Abel at second bases. Charlie grounds out, advancing Baker to second base. Daniel singles, scoring Baker. Baker's run is charged to Peter.

(3) Peter is pitching. Abel reaches first base on a base on balls. Roger relieves Peter. Baker singles, advancing Abel to third base. Charlie grounds to short, with Abel out at home plate and Baker advancing to second base. Daniel flies out. Edward singles, scoring Baker. Baker's run is charged to Peter.

(4) Peter is pitching. Abel reaches first base on a base on balls. Roger relieves Peter. Baker reaches on a base on balls. Charlie flies out. Abel is picked off second base. Daniel doubles, scoring Baker from first base. Baker's run is charged to Roger.

(5) Peter is pitching. Abel reaches first base on a base on balls. Roger relieves Peter. Baker reaches first base on a base on balls. Sierra relieves Roger. Charlie forces Abel at third base. Daniel forces Baker at third base. Edward hits a home run, scoring three runs. The Official Scorer shall charge one run to Peter, one run to Roger and one run to Sierra.

(6) Peter is pitching. Abel reaches first base on a base on balls. Roger relieves Peter. Baker reaches first base on a base on balls. Charlie singles, filling the bases. Daniel forces Abel at home plate. Edward singles, scoring Baker and Charlie. The Official Scorer shall charge one run to Peter and one run to Roger.

(7) Peter is pitching. Abel reaches first base on a base on balls. Roger relieves Peter. Baker singles, but Abel is out trying to reach third base and Baker advances to second base on the throw. Charlie singles, scoring Baker. Baker's run is charged to Roger.

(h) A relief pitcher shall not be held accountable when the first batter to whom he pitches reaches first base on four called balls if such batter has a decided advantage in the ball and strike count when pitchers are changed.

(1) If, when pitchers are changed, the count is

2 balls, no strike,

2 balls, 1 strike,

3 balls, no strike,

3 balls, 1 strike,

3 balls, 2 strikes,

and the batter gets a base on balls, the Official Scorer shall charge that batter and the base on balls to the preceding pitcher, not to the relief pitcher.

(2) Any other action by such batter, such as reaching base on a hit, an error, a fielder's choice, a force-out, or being touched by a pitched ball, shall cause such a batter to be charged to the relief pitcher.

Rule 9.16(h) Comment: The provisions of Rule 9.16(h)(2) shall not be construed as affecting or conflicting with the provisions of Rule 9.16(g).

(3) If, when pitchers are changed, the count is

2 balls, 2 strikes,

1 ball, 2 strikes,

1 ball, 1 strike,

1 ball, no strike,

no ball, 2 strikes,

no ball, 1 strike,

the Official Scorer shall charge that batter and the actions of that batter to the relief pitcher.

(i) When pitchers are changed during an inning, the relief pitcher shall not have the benefit of previous chances for outs not accepted in determining earned runs.

Rule 9.16(i) Comment: It is the intent of Rule 9.16(i) to charge a relief pitcher with earned runs for which such relief pitcher is solely responsible. In some instances, runs charged as earned against the relief pitcher can be charged as unearned against the team. For example:

(1) With two out and Peter pitching, Abel reaches first base on a base on balls. Baker reaches first base on an error. Roger relieves Peter. Charlie hits a home run, scoring three runs. The Official Scorer shall charge two unearned runs to Peter, one earned run to

Roger and three unearned runs to the team (because the inning should have ended with the third out when Baker batted and an error was committed).

(2) With two out, and Peter pitching, Abel and Baker each reach first base on a base on balls. Roger relieves Peter. Charlie reaches first base on an error. Daniel hits a home run, scoring four runs. The Official Scorer shall charge two unearned runs to Peter and two unearned runs to Roger (because the inning should have ended with the third out when Charlie batted and an error was committed).

(3) With none out and Peter pitching, Abel reaches first base on a base on balls. Baker reaches first base on an error. Roger relieves Peter. Charlie hits a home run, scoring three runs. Daniel and Edward strike out. Frank reaches first base on an error. George hits a home run, scoring two runs. The Official Scorer shall charge two runs, one of them earned, to Peter, three runs, one of them earned, to Roger and five runs, two of them earned, to the team (because only Abel and Charlie would have scored in an inning reconstructed without the errors).

9.17 Winning and Losing Pitcher

(a) The Official Scorer shall credit as the winning pitcher that pitcher whose team assumes a lead while such pitcher is in the game, or during the inning on offense in which such pitcher is removed from the game, and does not relinquish such lead, unless

(1) such pitcher is a starting pitcher and Rule 9.17(b) applies; or (2) Rule 9.17(c) applies.

Rule 9.17(a) Comment: Whenever the score is tied, the game becomes a new contest insofar as the winning pitcher is concerned. Once the opposing team assumes the lead, all pitchers who have pitched up to that point and have been replaced are excluded from being credited with the victory. If the pitcher against whose pitching the opposing team gained the lead continues to pitch until his team regains the lead, which it holds to the finish of the game, that pitcher shall be the winning pitcher.

(b) If the pitcher whose team assumes a lead while such pitcher is in the game, or during the inning on offense in which such pitcher is removed from the game, and does not relinquish such lead, is a starting pitcher who has not completed

    (1) five innings of a game that lasts six or more innings on defense, or

    (2) four innings of a game that lasts five innings on defense, then the Official Scorer shall credit as the winning pitcher the relief pitcher, if there is only one relief pitcher, or the relief pitcher who, in the Official Scorer's judgment was the most effective, if there is more than one relief pitcher.

Rule 9.17(b) Comment: It is the intent of Rule 9.17(b) that a relief pitcher pitch at least one complete inning or pitch when a crucial out is made, within the context of the game (including the score), in order to be credited as the winning pitcher. If the first relief pitcher pitches effectively, the Official Scorer should not presumptively credit that pitcher with the win, because the rule requires that the win be credited to the pitcher who was the most effective, and a subsequent relief pitcher may have been most effective. The Official Scorer, in determining which relief pitcher was the most effective, should consider the number of runs, earned runs and base runners given up by each relief pitcher and the context of the game at the time of each relief pitcher's appearance. If two or more relief pitchers were similarly effective, the Official Scorer should give the presumption to the earlier pitcher as the winning pitcher.

(c) The Official Scorer shall not credit as the winning pitcher a relief pitcher who is ineffective in a brief appearance, when at least one succeeding relief pitcher pitches effectively in helping his team maintain its lead. In such a case, the Official Scorer shall credit as the winning pitcher the succeeding relief pitcher who was most effective, in the judgment of the Official Scorer.

Rule 9.17(c) Comment: The Official Scorer generally should, but is not required to, consider the appearance of a relief pitcher to be ineffective and brief if such relief pitcher pitches less than one inning and allows two or more earned runs to score (even if such runs are charged to a previous pitcher). Rule 9.17(b) Comment provides guidance on choosing the winning pitcher from among several succeeding relief pitchers.

(d) A losing pitcher is a pitcher who is responsible for the run that gives the winning team a lead that the winning team does not relinquish.

Rule 9.17(d) Comment: Whenever the score is tied, the game becomes a new contest insofar as the losing pitcher is concerned.

(e) A league may designate a non-championship game (for example, the Major League All-Star Game) for which Rules 9.17(a)(1) and 9.17(b) do not apply. In such games, the Official Scorer shall credit as the winning pitcher that pitcher whose team assumes a lead while such pitcher is in the game, or during the inning on offense in which such pitcher is removed from the game, and does not relinquish such lead, unless such pitcher is knocked out after the winning team has attained a commanding lead and the Official Scorer concludes that a subsequent pitcher is entitled to credit as the winning pitcher.

9.18 Shutouts

A shutout is a statistic credited to a pitcher who allows no runs in a game. No pitcher shall be credited with pitching a shutout unless he pitches the complete game, or unless he enters the game with none out before the opposing team has scored in the first inning, puts out the side without a run scoring and pitches the rest of the game without allowing a run. When two or more pitchers combine to pitch a shutout, the league statistician shall make a notation to that effect in the league's official pitching records.

9.19 Saves for Relief Pitchers

A save is a statistic credited to a relief pitcher, as set forth in this Rule 9.19.

The Official Scorer shall credit a pitcher with a save when such pitcher meets all four of the following conditions:

(a) He is the finishing pitcher in a game won by his team;

(b) He is not the winning pitcher;

(c) He is credited with at least $\frac{1}{3}$ of an inning pitched; and

(d) He satisfies one of the following conditions:

> (1) He enters the game with a lead of no more than three runs and pitches for at least one inning;
>
> (2) He enters the game, regardless of the count, with the potential tying run either on base, or at bat or on deck (that is, the potential tying run is either already on base or is one of the first two batters he faces); or
>
> (3) He pitches for at least three innings.

9.20 Statistics

The Office of the Commissioner shall appoint an official statistician. The statistician shall maintain an accumulative record of all the batting, fielding, running and pitching records specified in Rule 9.02 for every player who appears in a league championship game or post-season game.

The statistician shall prepare a tabulated report at the end of the season, including all individual and team records for every championship game, and shall submit this report to the Office of the Commissioner. This report shall identify each player by his first name and surname and shall indicate as to each batter whether he bats righthanded, lefthanded or both ways, and as to each fielder and pitcher, whether he throws righthanded or lefthanded.

When a player listed in the starting lineup is substituted for before he plays on defense, he shall not receive credit in the defensive statistics (fielding) unless he actually plays that position during the game. All such players, however, shall be credited with one game played (in batting statistics) so long as they are announced into the game or listed on the official lineup card.

Rule 9.20 Comment: The Official Scorer shall credit a player with having played on defense if such player is on the field for at least one pitch or play. If a game is called (for example, because of rain) after a substitute player enters the field but before a pitch is thrown or a play is made, the Official Scorer shall credit such player with a game played in the batting statistics but shall not credit such player in any defensive statistics. If a game is called (for example, because of rain) after a relief pitcher enters the field but before a pitch is thrown or a play is made, the Official Scorer shall credit such pitcher with a game played in the batting statistics but shall not credit such pitcher in any defensive statistics or with a game pitched.

Any games played to break a divisional tie shall be included in the statistics for that championship season.

9.21 Determining Percentage Records

To compute:

(a) Percentage of games won and lost, divide the number of games won by the sum of games won and games lost;

(b) Batting average, divide the total number of safe hits (not the total bases on hits) by the total times at bat, as defined in Rule 9.02(a);

(c) Slugging percentage, divide the total bases of all safe hits by the total times at bat, as defined in Rule 9.02(a);

(d) Fielding average, divide the sum of putouts and assists by the sum of putouts, assists and errors (which shall be called chances);

(e) Pitcher's earned-run average, multiply the total earned runs charged against such pitcher by 9, and divide the result by the total number of innings he pitched, including fractions of an inning; and

Rule 9.21(e) Comment: For example, $9\frac{1}{3}$ innings pitched and 3 earned runs is an earned-run average of 2.89 (3 earned runs times 9 divided by $9\frac{1}{3}$ equals 2.89).

(f) On-base percentage (or on-base average), divide the sum of hits, bases on balls and times hit by pitch by the sum of at-bats, bases on balls, times hit by pitch and sacrifice flies.

Rule 9.21(f) Comment: For the purpose of computing on-base percentage, ignore instances of a batter being awarded first base on interference or obstruction.

9.22 Minimum Standards for Individual Championships

To assure uniformity in establishing the batting, pitching and fielding championships of professional leagues, such champions shall meet the following minimum performance standards:

(a) The individual batting, slugging or on-base percentage champion shall be the player with the highest batting average, slugging percentage or on-base percentage, as the case may be, provided the player is credited with as many or more total appearances at the plate in league championship games as the number of games scheduled for each Club in his Club's league that season, multiplied by 3.1 in the case of a Major League player and by 2.7 in the case of a Minor League player. Total appearances at the plate shall include official times at bat, plus bases on balls, times hit by pitcher, sacrifice hits, sacrifice flies and times awarded first base because of interference or obstruction. Notwithstanding the foregoing requirement of minimum appearances at the plate, any player with fewer than the required number of plate appearances whose average would be the highest, if he were charged with the required number of plate appearances shall be awarded the batting, slugging or on-base percentage championship, as the case may be.

Rule 9.22(a) Comment: For example, if a Major League schedules 162 games for each Club, 502 plate appearances qualify (162 times 3.1 equals 502) a player for a batting, slugging or on-base percentage championship. If 140 games are scheduled for each Club in a Minor League, 378 plate appearances qualify (140 times 2.7 equals 378) a player for a batting, slugging or on-base percentage championship. Fractions of a plate appearance are to be rounded up or down to the closest whole number. For example, 162 times 3.1 equals 502.2, which is rounded down to a requirement of 502.

If, for example, Abel has the highest batting average among those with 502 plate appearance in a Major League with a .362 batting average (181 hits in 500 at-bats), and Baker has 490 plate appearances, 440 at-bats and 165 hits for a .375 batting average, Baker shall be the batting champion, because adding 12 more at-bats to Baker's record would still give Baker a higher batting average than Abel: .365 (165 hits in 452 at-bats) to Abel's .362.

(b) The individual pitching champion in a Major League shall be the pitcher with the lowest earned-run average, provided that the pitcher has pitched at least as many innings in league championship games as the number of games scheduled for each Club in his Club's league that season. The individual pitching champion in a Minor League shall be the pitcher with the lowest earned-run average provided that the pitcher has pitched at least as many innings in league championship season games as 80% of the number of games scheduled for each Club in the pitcher's league.

Rule 9.22(b) Comment: For example, if a Major League schedules 162 games for each Club, 162 innings qualify a pitcher for a pitching championship. A pitcher with 161⅔ innings would not qualify. If 140 games are scheduled for each Club in a Minor League, 112 innings qualify a pitcher for a pitching championship. Fractions of an inning for the required number of innings are to be rounded to the closest third of an inning. For example, 80% of 144 games is 115.2, so 115⅓ innings would be the minimum required for a pitching championship in a Minor League with 144 games scheduled and 80% of 76 games is 60.8, so 60⅔ innings would be the minimum required for a pitching championship in a Minor League with 76 games scheduled.

(c) The individual fielding champions shall be the fielders with the highest fielding average at each position, provided:

(1) A catcher must have participated as a catcher in at least one-half the number of games scheduled for each Club in his league that season;

(2) An infielder or outfielder must have participated at his position in at least two-thirds of the number of games scheduled for each Club in his league that season; and

(3) A pitcher must have pitched at least as many innings as the number of games scheduled for each Club in his league that season, unless another pitcher has a fielding average

as high or higher and has handled more total chances in fewer innings, in which case such other pitcher shall be the fielding champion.

9.23 Guidelines for Cumulative Performance Records

(a) Consecutive Hitting Streaks

A consecutive hitting streak shall not be terminated if a batter's plate appearance results in a base on balls, hit batsman, defensive interference or obstruction or a sacrifice bunt. A sacrifice fly shall terminate the streak.

(b) Consecutive-Game Hitting Streaks

A consecutive-game hitting streak shall not be terminated if all of a batter's plate appearances (one or more) in a game result in a base on balls, hit batsman, defensive interference or obstruction or a sacrifice bunt. The streak shall terminate if the player has a sacrifice fly and no hit.

A player's individual consecutive-game hitting streak shall be determined by the consecutive games in which such player appears and is not determined by his Club's games.

(c) Consecutive-Game Playing Streak

A consecutive-game playing streak shall be extended if a player plays one half-inning on defense or if the player completes a time at bat by reaching base or being put out. A pinch-running appearance only shall not extend the streak. If a player is ejected from a game by an umpire before such player can comply with the requirements of this Rule 9.23(c), such player's streak shall continue.

(d) Suspended Games

For the purpose of this Rule 9.23 all performances in the completion of a suspended game shall be considered as occurring on the original date of the game.

DEFINITIONS OF TERMS
(All definitions are listed alphabetically)

ADJUDGED is a judgment decision by the umpire.

An APPEAL is the act of a fielder in claiming violation of the rules by the offensive team.

A BALK is an illegal act by the pitcher with a runner or runners on base, entitling all runners to advance one base.

A BALL is a pitch which does not enter the strike zone in flight and is not struck at by the batter. If the pitch touches the ground and bounces through the strike zone it is a "ball."

A BASE is one of four points which must be touched by a runner in order to score a run; more usually applied to the canvas bags and the rubber plate which mark the base points.

A BASE COACH is a team member in uniform who is stationed in the coach's box at first or third base to direct the batter and the runners.

A BASE ON BALLS is an award of first base granted to a batter who, during his time at bat, receives four pitches outside the strike zone or following a signal from the defensive team's manager to the umpire that he intends to intentionally walk the batter. If the manager informs the umpire of this intention, the umpire shall award the batter first base as if the batter had received four pitches outside the strike zone.

A BATTER is an offensive player who takes his position in the batter's box.

BATTER-RUNNER is a term that identifies the offensive player who has just finished his time at bat until he is put out or until the play on which he became a runner ends.

The BATTER'S BOX is the area within which the batter shall stand during his time at bat.

The BATTERY is the pitcher and catcher.

BENCH OR DUGOUT is the seating facilities reserved for players, substitutes and other team members in uniform when they are not actively engaged on the playing field.

145

Definitions of Terms

A BUNT is a batted ball not swung at, but intentionally met with the bat and tapped slowly within the infield.

A CALLED GAME is one in which, for any reason, the umpire-in-chief or the Office of the Commissioner terminates play before the game is completed.

A CATCH is the act of a fielder in getting secure possession in his hand or glove of a ball in flight and firmly holding it; providing he does not use his cap, protector, pocket or any other part of his uniform in getting possession. It is not a catch, however, if simultaneously or immediately following his contact with the ball, he collides with a player, or with a wall, or if he falls down, and as a result of such collision or falling, drops the ball. It is not a catch if a fielder touches a fly ball which then hits a member of the offensive team or an umpire and then is caught by another defensive player. In establishing the validity of the catch, the fielder shall hold the ball long enough to prove that he has complete control of the ball and that his release of the ball is voluntary and intentional. If the fielder has made the catch and drops the ball while in the act of making a throw following the catch, the ball shall be adjudged to have been caught.

(Catch) Comment: A catch is legal if the ball is finally held by any fielder, even though juggled, or held by another fielder before it touches the ground. Runners may leave their bases the instant the first fielder touches the ball. A fielder may reach over a fence, railing, rope or other line of demarcation to make a catch. He may jump on top of a railing, or canvas that may be in foul ground. No interference should be allowed when a fielder reaches over a fence, railing, rope or into a stand to catch a ball. He does so at his own risk.

If a fielder, attempting a catch at the edge of the dugout, is "held up" and kept from an apparent fall by a player or players of either team and the catch is made, it shall be allowed.

The CATCHER is the fielder who takes his position back of the home base.

The CATCHER'S BOX is that area within which the catcher shall stand until the pitcher delivers the ball.

Definitions of Terms

THE CLUB is a person or group of persons responsible for assembling the team personnel, providing the playing field and required facilities, and representing the team in relations with the league.

A COACH is a team member in uniform appointed by the manager to perform such duties as the manager may designate, such as but not limited to acting as base coach.

A DEAD BALL is a ball out of play because of a legally created temporary suspension of play.

The DEFENSE (or DEFENSIVE) is the team, or any player of the team, in the field.

A DOUBLE-HEADER is two regularly scheduled or rescheduled games, played in immediate succession.

A DOUBLE PLAY is a play by the defense in which two offensive players are put out as a result of continuous action, providing there is no error between putouts.

(a) A force double play is one in which both putouts are force plays.

(b) A reverse force double play is one in which the first out is a force play and the second out is made on a runner for whom the force is removed by reason of the first out. Examples of reverse force plays: runner on first, one out; batter grounds to first baseman, who steps on first base (one out) and throws to second baseman or shortstop for the second out (a tag play). Another example: bases loaded, none out; batter grounds to third baseman, who steps on third base (one out); then throws to catcher for the second out (tag play).

DUGOUT (*See* definition of BENCH)

A FAIR BALL is a batted ball that settles on fair ground between home and first base, or between home and third base, or that is on or over fair territory when bounding to the outfield past first or third base, or that touches first, second or third base, or that first falls on fair territory on or beyond first base or third base, or that, while on or over fair territory touches the person of an umpire or player, or that, while over fair territory, passes out of the playing field in flight.

Definitions of Terms

A fair fly shall be judged according to the relative position of the ball and the foul line, including the foul pole, and not as to whether the fielder is on fair or foul territory at the time he touches the ball.

> *(Fair Ball) Comment:* If a fly ball lands in the infield between home and first base, or home and third base, and then bounces to foul territory without touching a player or umpire and before passing first or third base, it is a foul ball; or if the ball settles on foul territory or is touched by a player on foul territory, it is a foul ball. If a fly ball lands on or beyond first or third base and then bounces to foul territory, it is a fair hit.
>
> A batted ball not touched by a fielder, which hits the pitcher's rubber and rebounds into foul territory, between home and first, or between home and third base is a foul ball.
>
> Clubs, increasingly, are erecting tall foul poles at the fence line with a wire netting extending along the side of the pole on fair territory above the fence to enable the umpires more accurately to judge fair and foul balls.

FAIR TERRITORY is that part of the playing field within, and including the first base and third base lines, from home base to the bottom of the playing field fence and perpendicularly upwards. All foul lines are in fair territory.

A FIELDER is any defensive player.

FIELDER'S CHOICE is the act of a fielder who handles a fair grounder and, instead of throwing to first base to put out the batter-runner, throws to another base in an attempt to put out a preceding runner. The term is also used by scorers (a) to account for the advance of the batter-runner who takes one or more extra bases when the fielder who handles his safe hit attempts to put out a preceding runner; (b) to account for the advance of a runner (other than by stolen base or error) while a fielder is attempting to put out another runner; and (c) to account for the advance of a runner made solely because of the defensive team's indifference (undefended steal).

A FLY BALL is a batted ball that goes high in the air in flight.

A FORCE PLAY is a play in which a runner legally loses his right to occupy a base by reason of the batter becoming a runner.

(Force Play) Comment: Confusion regarding this play is removed by remembering that frequently the "force" situation is removed during the play. Example: Man on first, one out, ball hit sharply to first baseman who touches the bag and batter-runner is out. The force is removed at that moment and runner advancing to second must be tagged. If there had been a runner on third or second, and either of these runners scored before the tag-out at second, the run counts. Had the first baseman thrown to second and the ball then had been returned to first, the play at second was a force out, making two outs, and the return throw to first ahead of the runner would have made three outs. In that case, no run would score.

Example: Not a force out. One out. Runner on first and third. Batter flies out. Two out. Runner on third tags up and scores. Runner on first tries to retouch before throw from fielder reaches first baseman, but does not get back in time and is out. Three outs. If, in umpire's judgment, the runner from third touched home before the ball was held at first base, the run counts.

A FORFEITED GAME is a game declared ended by the umpire-in-chief in favor of the offended team by the score of 9 to 0, for violation of the rules.

A FOUL BALL is a batted ball that settles on foul territory between home and first base, or between home and third base, or that bounds past first or third base on or over foul territory, or that first falls on foul territory beyond first or third base, or that, while on or over foul territory, touches the person of an umpire or player, or any object foreign to the natural ground.

A foul fly shall be judged according to the relative position of the ball and the foul line, including the foul pole, and not as to whether the infielder is on foul or fair territory at the time he touches the ball.

(Foul Ball) Comment: A batted ball not touched by a fielder, which hits the pitcher's rubber and rebounds into foul territory, between home and first, or between home and third base is a foul ball.

If a fly ball lands in the infield between home and first base, or home and third base, and then bounces to foul territory without touching a player or umpire and before passing first or third base, it is a foul ball; or if the ball settles on foul territory or is touched by a player on foul territory, it is a foul ball. If a fly ball lands on or beyond first or third base and then bounces to foul territory, it is a fair hit.

FOUL TERRITORY is that part of the playing field outside the first and third base lines extended to the fence and perpendicularly upwards.

A FOUL TIP is a batted ball that goes sharp and direct from the bat to the catcher and is legally caught. It is not a foul tip unless caught, and any foul tip that is caught is a strike, and the ball is in play.

A GROUND BALL is a batted ball that rolls or bounces close to the ground.

The HOME TEAM is the team on whose grounds the game is played, or if the game is played on neutral grounds, the home team shall be designated by mutual agreement.

ILLEGAL (or ILLEGALLY) is contrary to these rules.

An ILLEGAL PITCH is (1) a pitch delivered to the batter when the pitcher does not have his pivot foot in contact with the pitcher's plate; (2) a quick return pitch. An illegal pitch when runners are on base is a balk.

An INFIELDER is a fielder who occupies a position in the infield.

An INFIELD FLY is a fair fly ball (not including a line drive nor an attempted bunt) which can be caught by an infielder with ordinary effort, when first and second, or first, second and third bases are occupied, before two are out. The pitcher, catcher and any outfielder who stations himself in the infield on the play shall be considered infielders for the purpose of this rule.

When it seems apparent that a batted ball will be an Infield Fly, the umpire shall immediately declare "Infield Fly" for the benefit of the runners. If the ball is near the baselines, the umpire shall declare "Infield Fly, if Fair."

The ball is alive and runners may advance at the risk of the ball being caught, or retouch and advance after the ball is touched, the same as on any fly ball. If the hit becomes a foul ball, it is treated the same as any foul.

If a declared Infield Fly is allowed to fall untouched to the ground, and bounces foul before passing first or third base, it is a foul ball. If a declared Infield Fly falls untouched to the ground outside the baseline, and bounces fair before passing first or third base, it is an Infield Fly.

(Infield Fly) Comment: On the infield fly rule the umpire is to rule whether the ball could ordinarily have been handled by an infielder-not by some arbitrary limitation such as the grass, or the base lines. The umpire must rule also that a ball is an infield fly, even if handled by an outfielder, if, in the umpire's judgment, the ball could have been as easily handled by an infielder. The infield fly is in no sense to be considered an appeal play. The umpire's judgment must govern, and the decision should be made immediately.

When an infield fly rule is called, runners may advance at their own risk. If on an infield fly rule, the infielder intentionally drops a fair ball, the ball remains in play despite the provisions of Rule 5.09(a)(12). The infield fly rule takes precedence.

If interference is called during an Infield Fly, the ball remains alive until it is determined whether the ball is fair or foul. If fair, both the runner who interfered with the fielder and the batter are out. If foul, even if caught, the runner is out and the batter returns to bat.

IN FLIGHT describes a batted, thrown, or pitched ball which has not yet touched the ground or some object other than a fielder.

IN JEOPARDY is a term indicating that the ball is in play and an offensive player may be put out.

An INNING is that portion of a game within which the teams alternate on offense and defense and in which there are three putouts for each team. Each team's time at bat is a half-inning.

INTERFERENCE

(a) Offensive interference is an act by the team at bat which interferes with, obstructs, impedes, hinders or confuses any fielder attempting to make a play.

Definitions of Terms

(b) Defensive interference is an act by a fielder that hinders or prevents a batter from hitting a pitch.

(c) Umpire's interference occurs (1) when a plate umpire hinders, impedes or prevents a catcher's throw attempting to prevent a stolen base or retire a runner on a pick-off play, or (2) when a fair ball touches an umpire on fair territory before passing a fielder.

(d) Spectator interference occurs when a spectator (or an object thrown by the spectator) hinders a player's attempt to make a play on a live ball, by going onto the playing field, or reaching out of the stands and over the playing field.

THE LEAGUE is a group of Clubs whose teams play each other in a pre-arranged schedule under these rules for the league championship.

LEGAL (or LEGALLY) is in accordance with these rules.

A LIVE BALL is a ball which is in play.

A LINE DRIVE is a batted ball that goes sharp and direct from the bat to a fielder without touching the ground.

THE MANAGER is a person appointed by the Club to be responsible for the team's actions on the field, and to represent the team in communications with the umpire and the opposing team. A player may be appointed manager.

MINOR LEAGUE shall refer to any league within the professional development league system operated by Major League Baseball in which Minor League Clubs are assigned to compete.

MINOR LEAGUE CLUB shall refer to any professional baseball club that is party to a Player Development License Agreement ("PDL").

OBSTRUCTION is the act of a fielder who, while not in possession of the ball and not in the act of fielding the ball, impedes the progress of any runner.

OFFENSE is the team, or any player of the team, at bat.

OFFICIAL SCORER. *See* Rule 9.00.

ORDINARY EFFORT is the effort that a fielder of average skill at a position in that league or classification of leagues should exhibit on a play, with due consideration given to the condition of the field and weather conditions.

> *(Ordinary Effort) Comment:* This standard, called for several times in the Official Scoring Rules (e.g., Rules 9.05(a)(3), 9.05(a)(4), 9.05(a)(6), 9.05(b)(3) (Base Hits); 9.08(b) (Sacrifices); 9.12(a)(1) Comment, 9.12(d)(2) (Errors); and 9.13(a), 9.13(b) (Wild Pitches and Passed Balls)) and in the Official Baseball Rules (e.g., Definitions of Terms, Infield Fly), is an objective standard in regard to any particular fielder. In other words, even if a fielder makes his best effort, if that effort falls short of what an average fielder at that position in that league would have made in a situation, the Official Scorer should charge that fielder with an error.

An OUT is one of the three required retirements of an offensive team during its time at bat.

An OUTFIELDER is a fielder who occupies a position in the outfield, which is the area of the playing field most distant from home base.

OVERSLIDE (or OVERSLIDING) is the act of an offensive player when his slide to a base, other than when advancing from home to first base, is with such momentum that he loses contact with the base.

A PENALTY is the application of these rules following an illegal act.

The PERSON of a player or an umpire is any part of his body, his clothing or his equipment.

A PITCH is a ball delivered to the batter by the pitcher.

> *(Pitch) Comment:* All other deliveries of the ball by one player to another are thrown balls.

A PITCHER is the fielder designated to deliver the pitch to the batter.

The pitcher's PIVOT FOOT is that foot which is in contact with the pitcher's plate as he delivers the pitch.

"PLAY" is the umpire's order to start the game or to resume action following any dead ball.

Definitions of Terms

A POSTPONED GAME is one in which, for any reason, the game is not commenced on the day it was scheduled.

A QUICK RETURN pitch is one made with obvious intent to catch a batter off balance. It is an illegal pitch.

REGULATION GAME *See* Rule 7.01.

A RETOUCH is the act of a runner in returning to a base as legally required.

A RUN (or SCORE) is the score made by an offensive player who advances from batter to runner and touches first, second, third and home bases in that order.

A RUN-DOWN is the act of the defense in an attempt to put out a runner between bases.

A RUNNER is an offensive player who is advancing toward, or touching, or returning to any base.

"SAFE" is a declaration by the umpire that a runner is entitled to the base for which he was trying.

SET POSITION is one of the two legal pitching positions.

SQUEEZE PLAY is a term to designate a play when a team, with a runner on third base, attempts to score that runner by means of a bunt.

A STRIKE is a legal pitch when so called by the umpire, which:

(a) Is struck at by the batter and is missed;

(b) Is not struck at, if any part of the ball passes through any part of the strike zone;

(c) Is fouled by the batter when he has less than two strikes;

(d) Is bunted foul;

(e)Touches the batter as he strikes at it;

(f) Touches the batter in flight in the strike zone; or

(g) Becomes a foul tip.

The STRIKE ZONE is that area over home plate the upper limit of which is a horizontal line at the midpoint between the top of the shoulders and the top of the uniform pants, and the lower level is a line at the hollow

154

beneath the kneecap. The Strike Zone shall be determined from the batter's stance as the batter is prepared to swing at a pitched ball. (For diagram of STRIKE ZONE, *see* Appendix 5.)

A SUSPENDED GAME is a called game which is to be completed at a later date.

A TAG is the action of a fielder in touching a base with his body while holding the ball securely and firmly in his hand or glove; or touching a runner with the ball, or with his hand or glove holding the ball (not including hanging laces alone), while holding the ball securely and firmly in his hand or glove. It is not a tag, however, if simultaneously or immediately following his touching a base or touching a runner, the fielder drops the ball. In establishing the validity of the tag, the fielder shall hold the ball long enough to prove that he has complete control of the ball. If the fielder has made a tag and drops the ball while in the act of making a throw following the tag, the tag shall be adjudged to have been made. For purposes of this definition any jewelry being worn by a player (e.g., necklaces, bracelets, etc.) shall not constitute a part of the player's body.

A THROW is the act of propelling the ball with the hand and arm to a given objective and is to be distinguished, always, from the pitch.

A TIE GAME is a regulation game which is called when each team has the same number of runs.

"TIME" is the announcement by an umpire of a legal interruption of play, during which the ball is dead.

TOUCH. To touch a player or umpire is to touch any part of his body, or any uniform or equipment worn by him (but not any jewelry (e.g., necklaces, bracelets, etc.) worn by a player).

(Touch) Comment: Equipment shall be considered worn by a player or umpire if it is in contact with its intended place on his person.

A TRIPLE PLAY is a play by the defense in which three offensive players are put out as a result of continuous action, providing there is no error between putouts.

Definitions of Terms

WILD PITCH is one so high, so low, or so wide of the plate that it cannot be handled with ordinary effort by the catcher.

WIND-UP POSITION is one of the two legal pitching positions.

NOTE: Any reference in these Official Baseball Rules to "he," "him" or "his" shall be deemed to be a reference to "she," "her" or "hers," as the case may be, when the person is a female.

APPENDICES

Appendix 1

Diagram No. 1
Diagram of the Playing Field

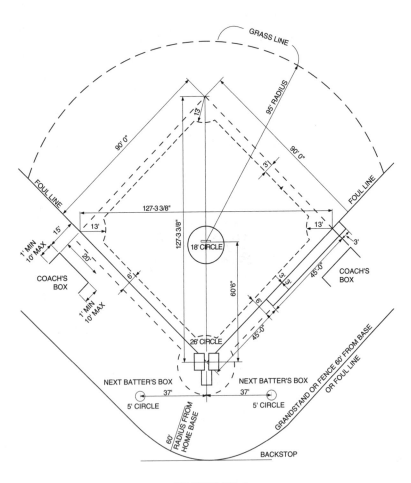

DIAGRAM NO. 1

LEGEND

——— BATTER'S BOX,
CATCHER'S BOX, FOUL LINE,
PITCHER'S PLATE, COACH'S BOX
◯ NEXT BATTER'S BOX
– – – – – BASE LINES
— — — GRASS LINES

Rev2018TL

Appendix 2

Diagram No. 2
Layout at Home Plate, 1st, 2nd, and 3rd Bases

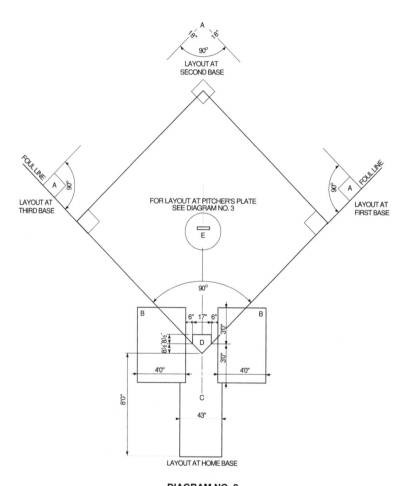

DIAGRAM NO. 2

LEGEND

A   1st, 2nd, 3rd BASES
B   BATTER'S BOX
C   CATCHER'S BOX
D   HOME BASE
E   PITCHER'S PLATE

Rev2023RW

Appendix 3

Diagram No. 3
Layout of Pitching Mound

Suggested Layout of Pitching Mound

This Diagram No. 3 supplements and, in cases of difference, supersedes Diagram No. 2.

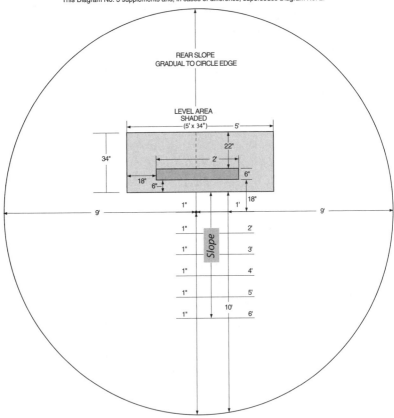

DIAGRAM NO. 3

Pitching Mound: An 18' diameter circle, center of which is 59' from back of home plate.

Locate front edge of rubber 18" behind center of mound.

Front edge of rubber to back point of home plate, 60'6".

Slope starts 6" from front edge of rubber.

The degree of slope from a starting point 6" in front of the pitcher's plate to a point 6' toward home plate shall be 1" to 1', and such degree of slope shall be uniform.

Level area surrounding rubber should be 6" in front of rubber, 18" to each side and 22" to rear of rubber. Total level area 5' x 34".

160

Appendix 4

Dimensions of Fielder's Glove

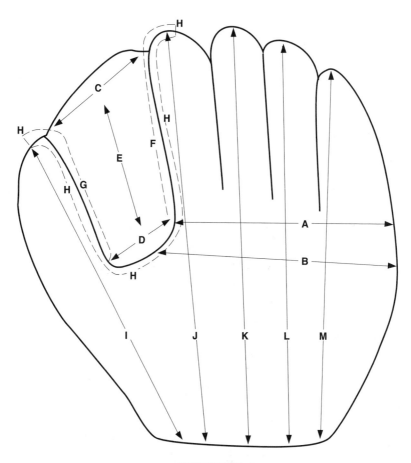

DIAGRAM NO. 4

(A) Palm width—7³/₄"
(B) Palm width—8"
(C) Top opening of web—4¹/₂"
(webbing not to be wider
than 4¹/₂" at any point)
(D) Bottom opening of web—3¹/₂"
(E) Web top to bottom—5³/₄"
(F) 1st finger crotch seam—5¹/₂"
(G) Thumb crotch seam—5¹/₂"

(H) Crotch seam—13³/₄"
(I) Thumb top to bottom edge—7³/₄"
(J) 1st finger top to bottom edge—13"
(K) 2nd finger top to bottom edge—11³/₄"
(L) 3rd finger top to bottom edge—10³/₄"
(M) 4th finger to bottom edge—9"

161

Appendix 5

The Strike Zone

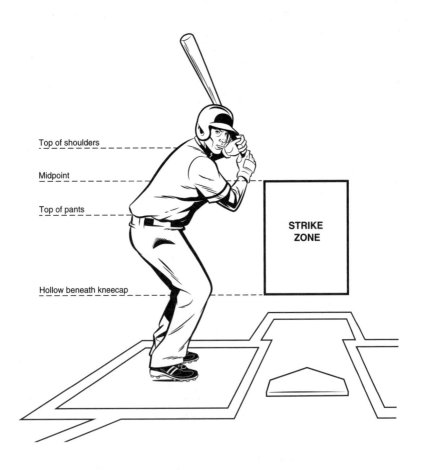

Top of shoulders

Midpoint

Top of pants

STRIKE
ZONE

Hollow beneath kneecap

Index

Rules 1.00 through 8.00

Note: For any items not listed and for additional information, see alphabetized entries in Definitions of Terms.

Index

Base on Balls (Automatic by Manager's Signal)—
Definitions of Terms ("Base on Balls"), 5.05(b)(1) Comment.

Base Coaches—5.03;
Helmets 3.08(e);
Interference 6.01(a)(8-9), 6.01(b), 6.01(d), 6.01(f);
Restrictions 5.03(a-c), 5.03 PENALTY, 5.10(k), 6.04(a).

Bat—3.02;
Altered 6.03(a)(4).

Bat Boy/Girl—3.08(f), 4.07(a), 5.10(k).

Batter/Batter-Runner—
Backswing strikes catcher 6.03(a)(3);
Batter becomes a runner 5.05
Fails to advance to first base 5.05(a)(2), 5.05(b);
Hit by pitch 5.05(b)(2), 5.06(c)(1), 5.09(a)(6), Definitions of Terms ("Ball," "Strike");
Illegal action 6.03;
Interference by 5.09(a)(7-9,11), 5.09(b)(8), 6.01(a), 6.03(a)(3-4); 6.03(a)(3 and 4) EXCEPTION and Comment.
Interference with 5.05(b)(3), 5.06(b)(3)(D);
Interferes with catcher after dropped third strike 6.01(a)(1), 6.01(a)(1) Comment;
Position in batter's box Definitions of Terms, 5.04(b), 5.04(b)(4-5), 6.03(a)(1-3);
Struck by batted ball 5.05(b)(2) Comment, 5.06(c)(6)(1), 5.09(a)(7), 6.01(a)(11).

Batter's Box—2.01, Definitions of Terms, 5.04(b), 6.03(a), Appendix 2.

Batter's Box Rule—5.04(b).
NAPBL Regulations—5.04(b)(2) Comment, 5.04(b)(4).

Batting Order—4.03, 5.04(a), 5.10(a-f,j), 8.03(a)(8).

Batting Out of Order—6.03(b).

Bench/Dugout—2.05, Definitions of Terms.
Catch/Play attempts Definitions of Terms ("Catch" Comment), 5.06(b)(3)(C), 5.09(a)(1) Comment, 5.12(b)(6), 6.01(b);
Equipment 3.10;

Index

Sleeves 3.03(e);

Throws glove at ball (detached equipment) 5.06(b)(3)(E), 5.06(b)(4)(A-E).

Fielder's Choice—Definitions of Terms, 9.12(f)(2).

"Flying Start" by Runner—5.09(c)(1) Comment.

Force Play/Force Out—Definitions of Terms, 5.09(b)(6); Reinstated 5.09(b)(6).

Forfeit—4.07(b), 4.08(g), 4.07(b), 7.03, 8.03(a)(6), 9.03(e).

Foul Ball—Definitions of Terms, 5.06(c)(5), 5.09(a)(7-8).

Foul Tip—Definitions of Terms, 5.06(c)(7) Comment, 5.09(a)(2) Comment, 5.09(b)(5) Comment.

Fraternization—4.06.

Game-Ending Runs—5.08(b), 5.09(b)(1,2) Comment, 5.09(c) Comment, 7.01(g)(3).

Glove/Mitt—3.04, 3.05, 3.06, 3.07; Illegally touches live ball 5.06(b)(4)(A,C,E).

Ground Rules—4.05, 8.03(a)(9).

Groundskeepers—4.03(e), 4.08(g), 7.03(c).

Helmet—3.08, 5.09(a)(8) Comment.

Hidden Ball Trick—6.02(a)(9).

Home Run—5.05(a)(5,9), 5.06(b)(4)(A).

Illegal Bat—3.02, 6.03(a)(5), 6.03(a)(5) Comment.

Illegal Pitch—Definitions of Terms (Illegal Pitch and Quick Return), 5.07(a)(2) Comment, 6.02(a)(5), 6.02(b).

Illegally Batted Ball—5.06(c)(4), 6.03(a)(1).

Infield Fly—Definitions of Terms, 5.09(a)(5,12), 5.09(b)(7) Exception; Strikes runner (on or off base) 5.09(b)(7), 5.09(b)(7) Exception.

Intentional Walk (Automatic by Manager's Signal)—Definitions of Terms ("Base on Balls"), 5.05(b)(1) Comment; How Official Scorer Notates 9.14(d).

Intentionally Dropped Ball—5.09(a)(12).

Intentional Pitch at Batter—6.02(c)(9).

Interference—

Authorized on-field personnel 4.07(a);

167

Index

"Backswing" (Follow-Through) 6.03(a)(3) Comment;

Batter's 5.09(a)(8), 5.09(b)(8), 6.01(a)(3);

By batter after dropped third strike 6.01(a)(1), 6.01(a)(1) Comment;

Catcher's 5.05(b)(3), 5.06(b)(3)(D,E), 6.01(g);

Coach's 6.01(a)(8), 6.01(d) Comment, 6.01(f);

Defensive Definitions of Terms, 5.05(b)(3), 5.06(b)(3), 6.01(d,g);

Intentional (Double Play) 5.09(a)(13), 5.09(a)(13) Comment, 5.09(b)(3), 6.01(a)(6-7), 6.01(j);

Offensive Definitions of Terms, 5.05(b)(4), 5.06(c)(6-7), 5.09(a)(8-9,13-15), 5.09(b)(3,7-8,13), 6.01(a-b,d), 6.03(a)(3);

Runner struck by batted ball 5.05(a)(4), 5.05(b)(4), 5.06(c)(6), 5.09(b)(7), 6.01(a)(11);

Spectator Definitions of Terms (Interference(d)), 6.01(e);

Umpire Definitions of Terms, 5.05(b)(4), 5.06(c)(2-6);

While in contact with base 6.01(a)(1) Comment;

see also Base Coaches, Batter and Catcher.

Jewelry—5.05(b)(2) Comment, Definition of Terms ("Tag," "Touch.")

Length Between Doubleheaders—4.08(c).

Limitations on Visits to the Mound Per Game—5.10(m).

Light Failure—5.12(b), 7.02(a).

Lineup Cards—4.03, 5.11(a)(1,11).

Lodged Ball—5.05(a)(7), 5.06(b)(4)(F-G,I), 5.06(c)(7), 5.09(a)(2) Comment.

Missed Base or Home Plate—5.06(b)(4)(I) Comment, 5.09(b)(12), 5.09(c)(2-4);

see also Appeals and Runner (Touch requirements).

"No Game"—4.04(c), 7.01(e).

Obstruction—Definitions of Terms, 6.01(a)(10) Comment, 6.01(h);

By spectators 5.08(b) Comment.

Official Scorer—5.10(d), 8.03(a)(8);

Demeanor towards 9.01(a), 9.01(c);

Notating intentional walk by manager's signal 9.14(d);

see also Definitions of Terms and Rule 9.00.

Overrunning/Oversliding—

First base, 5.09(b)(4,6,11), 5.09(c)(3);

Home plate 5.09(b)(12), 5.09(c)(4).

"Overzealous Runner"—5.06(b)(3)(B) Comment.

Pinch-Hitter/Runner—*see* Substitutions.

Pitch—

Ball Definitions of Terms;

Pitcher delivery time limit 5.07(c);

Goes out of play 5.06(b)(4)(H);

Intentionally thrown at batter 6.02(c)(9);

Lodges in catcher's or umpire's equipment 5.06(b)(4)(I), 5.06(c)(7);

Strike Definitions of Terms;

Touches batter 5.05(b)(2), 5.06(c)(1), 5.09(a)(6), Definitions of Terms (Ball, Strike);

Touches runner attempting to score 5.06(c)(8), 5.09(a)(14).

Pitcher—

Altered baseball 3.01, 6.02(c)(2-7);

Ambidextrous 5.07(f);

Becomes infielder 5.07(e);

Changes to defensive position 5.10(d) Comment;

Delivery restrictions 5.07(a);

Delivery time limit 5.07(c);

Injured 5.07(b,f), 5.10(d) Comment, 5.10(f-g);

Intentionally pitches at batter 6.02(c)(9);

Legal position 5.07(a)(1-2);

Length of time for warm-up pitches between innings 5.07(b);

Limitations on warm-up pitches 5.07(b);

Minimum number of batters to face (NAPBL rule only) 5.10(g);

Mouth, goes to on mound 6.02(c)(1);

Pitcher delays 5.07(c);

Pitcher visits by manager or coach 5.10(l);

Pivot foot Definitions of Terms, 5.07(a)(1-2); 5.07(a)(2) Comment, 5.07(e);

Index

Possesses foreign object or substance 6.02(c)(7);
Preparatory pitches 5.07(b), 5.10(*l*) Comment;
Sleeves 3.03(e);
Throws out of play from pitcher's plate 5.06(b)(4)(H);
Warm-up pitches 5.07(b), 5.10(*l*) Comment.
Pitcher's Plate—2.01, 2.04.
Player or Umpire Incapacitated—5.10(f-g,i), 5.12(b)(3,8).
Player Restrictions—
Barred from stands 4.06;
Confined to bench 5.10(k);
Fraternizing 4.06;
General conduct 5.10(b) Comment, 6.04(a,d-e);
Placing ball inside uniform 5.06(c)(7) Comment.
Playing Field—2.01.
Police Protection—4.07(b).
Postponed Game—Definition of Terms
Postponement Responsibility—4.04.
Pregame Conference—4.03.
Protested Game—7.04, 8.02(b).
Quick Pitch—Definitions of Terms (Illegal Pitch, Quick Return), 5.07(a)(3), 6.02(a)(2) Comment, 6.02(b).
Rain Delays—4.03(e), 4.03 Comment.
Regulation Game—1.06, 7.01, 7.01(g), 7.02;
7-inning Game 7.01(a) Exception.
Rosin Bag—4.01(f), 6.02(d) Comment.
Runner—
Abandons effort to run bases 5.05(a)(2) Comment, 5.05(b), 5.09(b)(2, 11), 5.09(c)(3);
Advancing or returning after being put out—6.01(a)(5) Comment.
Entitled to base 5.06(a)(1-2), 6.01(a) Comment;
"Flying Start" when tagging up 5.09(c)(1) Comment;
Injured 5.12(b)(3)(A);
Intentionally crashing into catcher 6.01(i)(1);

170

Index

Index

Index

Notes

Notes

Notes

Notes

Notes

Notes

Notes